LEARNING
the
VOCABULARY of GOD

A Spiritual Diary

by
FRANK C. LAUBACH

Martino Publishing
Mansfield Centre, CT
2012

Martino Publishing
P.O. Box 373,
Mansfield Centre, CT 06250 USA

ISBN 978-1-61427-368-4

© 2012 Martino Publishing

Cover design by T. Matarazzo

Printed in the United States of America On 100% Acid-Free Paper

LEARNING
the
VOCABULARY OF GOD

A Spiritual Diary

by
FRANK C. LAUBACH

THE UPPER ROOM
The World's Most Widely Used Devotional Guide
and
Other Devotional Literature
1908 GRAND AVENUE
NASHVILLE 5, TENNESSEE

UR-90-15-0256
Printed in the United States of America

Learning the Vocabulary of God

A Spiritual Diary

By FRANK C. LAUBACH

Preface

ONE supreme problem for each man is how to live each day nobly, how to make the most out of the day so that no gap or chasm will yawn between the real and the ideal, as it does yawn in the low days of most men. We can help one another, can we not, by revealing how we are struggling to make our days sublime? We sin against one another, do we not, when we conceal our best under a plea of shyness or reticense? The chief inspirations in our lives are the examples of earnest, striving men and women, are they not—Paul, Thomas à Kempis, Stanley Jones, Sherwood Eddy, John Mott, who in turn drew from the perfect life of Christ?

Ask God, "How can I do the most for the world?" and will He not answer, "Live the most Christlike life you can, and let men see it"?

As a father who entertains high hopes for his son, I pass on this diary of my struggles for the noble life to you, my son Bob, and to any other sons who may, by chance, see what I have written here.

THE SALUTATION OF THE DAWN

Listen to the Exhortation of the Dawn!
Look to this day!
For it is Life, the very Life of Life.
In its brief course lie all the
Verities and Realities of your Existence:
The Bliss of Growth,

3

The Glory of Action,
  The Splendor of Beauty:
For yesterday is but a Dream,
And To-morrow is only a Vision:
But to-day well-lived makes
Every Yesterday a Dream of Happiness,
And every To-morrow a Vision of Hope.
Look well, therefore, to this day.
Such is the Salutation of the Dawn!
                    —*From the Sanskrit*

January, 1937

FRIDAY 1

GOD, I want to give You every minute of this year. I shall try to keep You in mind every moment of my waking hours. I shall try to let my hand write what You direct. I shall try to let You be the speaker and direct every word. I shall try to let You direct my acts. I shall try to learn Your language as it was taught by Jesus and all others through whom you speak—in beauty and singing birds and cool breezes, in radiant Christlike faces, in sacrifices and in tears. It will cost not only much, but *everything that conflicts with* this resolve.

—— • ——

SATURDAY 2

GOD, since every minute this year is to be directed by You, I must learn Your language. I must study Your full vocabulary. What I hear and see and feel today that would have been meaningless yesterday must now reveal Your meaning. A pain in my left arm and occasionally over my heart are Your voice saying that there are no minutes to be wasted away from You.

I am surprised at miracles which seem already to be happening. Meeting with Agatha Harrison and Mrs. Carl Heath seems to be a miracle. They will introduce me to the women's organizations of India and to the Indian Congress through Nehru.

"Take heed how ye hear."

SUNDAY 3

GOD, waiting for this motor to start, surrounded by people who are waiting for motors and talking in an unknown tongue, what are You saying? If I try to hear You in all this sound and color, I am as bewildered as when I try to understand these men and women speaking Hindi. Perhaps I shall one day understand both You and them. In all this crowd I found only one interpreter to tell me how much to pay. Do I need an interpreter for Your language? O Christ, Your lovely words, Your lovely deeds are not beyond my understanding. And when I think of You, Your love begins to burn in my heart. I must be like You, seeking need and trying to help every minute. I have tried in vain to know why need exists. But this I know and it is enough: that I must seek need, and love and help.

——— • ———

MONDAY 4

Baroda Bazaar

GOD, if You rule every movement, You will be inside my eyes directing them. The eyes are the windows of the soul. If You are in my eyes, men will see You there and call You *Love*. Then my life will be love with a picture of Christ in the center; Christ bearing a cross and wearing thorns, and with anguish in His heart. *That* love will bless everybody and harm nobody.

As my hostess read the Bible and prayed, I heard You speaking this morning. She was the channel broadcasting Your words. I shall try to listen for Your speaking through the language of men, especially men who are trying to do Your will.

6

TUESDAY 5

GOD, teach me how to hold on to You when thronged by people who are interested in other subjects more than in You. Help me today to increase my knowledge of Your vocabulary. As we have to learn a few words each day, what will these new words be today? Over three hundred and thirty millions who cannot read are calling for help. Need is Your language, is a word from You. How to approach this problem is baffling. Unsolved problems are Your language, for in them You are our schoolmaster training us to be Your children. I thank You for the call to share a real need with You. You teach by the project method!

———— • ————

WEDNESDAY 6

GOD, this prayer calendar says, "We sometimes fail because we imagine God is not interested in the little things. We are bidden to take *everything* to God." That would mean every movement of the hand. I *have* found, of late, that I write better if I ask You to flow through my hand. I have found that if I pray when I have lost something, You usually guide me straight to it. Not always, but I think whenever necessary.

This seeking to learn Your vocabulary seems to be the clue! Every hour is new evidence that You are trying to speak. This morning the prayer calendar asked, "How many messages have you had from God?" *That* was a message from God! You speak from the pages of books.

———— • ————

THURSDAY 7

GOD, this going in search of Your vocabulary promises to open a whole *world* of new vision. I have a little book in

7

my pocket to record Your words as they come to me all
day long, just as I might learn any language. Yesterday I
heard You speak and saw You write in conscience, pain,
loneliness, the breeze, a woven mat. These said, "Cooperate
with God." A half-naked child, the blue heaven, a slow
carabao, memories of early life (the past is Your voice);
my dead friends, especially my father who passed over last
year but seems to be here; poor eyes, failures, dreams, two
mottoes on the walls, the silence, piano music, the radio,
rippling water, a radiant smile of love—these, too, are words
God spoke.

———— • ————

FRIDAY 8

Baroda Bazaar

, GOD, we often open doors and find we have stepped into
heaven. Last night I asked the Koenigs for piano music
because I had heard the children playing. Mr. and Mrs.
Koenig played Beethoven's *Fifth Symphony* as I had never
heard it before. Every note was Your music for me. We
find You by opening the right doors.

Evidently this experiment in keeping You every moment
in mind is not new. The prayer calendar this morning says:
"We ought, in the secret of our hearts, to be communing
with God, our Father, all day long, hearing His voice, asking
His guidance." As we advance in acquaintance with God,
we shall have more of the spirit of little children—putting
all our trust in Him.

———— • ————

SATURDAY 9

Calcutta

GOD, this attempt to keep my *will* bent toward Your will
is integrating me. Here in this Calcutta station, I feel new
power such as I have not had for many years. The task to
which You have called me is as hard to accomplish as scaling

Mount Everest, but You can accomplish it if I can keep my will attuned to Your will. My task is a simple one, after all. It is just to guard this will. Religion seems to me today to be not doctrine or faith, primarily, but primarily the directed will. *That is my* task, to hold my will to the current of power, and let You sweep through endlessly.

——— • ———

SUNDAY 10

Santiniketan

GOD, Your mind is superior to mine in one tremendous particular: You will never forget me, or any other, because You can think of countless billions of subjects at the same instant. I try to keep You in mind every second, but I can think of only one set of things in an instant. My effort results in a succession of spasmodic starts with You and wanderings into other thoughts which leave You out. Perhaps I may need to keep a score based upon how frequently I come back to You for directions. It *does* make me feel *at home* to return to You and whisper "Father" in your ear every minute. This titanic task You led me to attack calls out *will* and a surging sense of power. We must lift heavy weights if we are to become strong.

——— • ———

MONDAY 11

Santiniketan

GOD, what is a man's best gift to mankind? To be beautiful of soul and then let people see into your soul—this is what I learned as I looked upon the face of Rabindranath Tagore and listened to him tell of his school and his ideals. His beautiful face reminded me of Moses. I tried to think of You every moment and to let You look through my eyes. His long, friendly response leads me to believe he saw You.

I must talk to others about You more than I have done. I can neither help them nor discover their deepest best unless

9

I reveal this fellowship with You to everybody. To meet You every minute of every day and to share You with others is to live a full life. What new miracle will enrich this day?

————— • —————

TUESDAY 12

Santiniketan

GOD, last night in the clear, dry air of India I saw the sun for the first time. Behind the western trees it was a terrible, immense circle of fiery flame one hundred thousand miles across. It blinded and fascinated me. So far away! And yet it seemed just over the edge of the world. Then I studied the stars and *saw* for the first time the vast difference in distance between Venus and some star near by. That sky full of those stupendous fiery furies like our sun! And for You all these dizzy distances are but spans of the hand. My Earth is but a speck and I less than an electron. Yet among the electrons You are at home as easily as along the mighty reaches of the universe, and at home in whatever may be beyond. After all, I cannot comprehend You. But if You are love, I can relax and not fear for today or eternity. *All.mighty!*

————— • —————

WEDNESDAY 13

Calcutta

THIS search for the vocabulary of God gives new meaning to many Bible verses. Open before me are the words of Luke 8:18 and 21: "Take heed therefore how ye hear" and "My mother and my brethren are these which hear the word of God, and do it." "Hear God and do it" is the center of this year's effort to hear and do, *every* instant of my waking day. To hear and do *perfectly* would be like Jesus. It would mean purity in the deep recesses of thought. I witness to any person who may read this spiritual diary that I am astonished

10

at the rich new inspiration which now floods my mind with fresh glorious vision from Heaven. I wrote a chapter yesterday on learning the vocabulary of God. Will it become a book, dear Father?

—— • ——

THURSDAY 14

Calcutta

GOD, this Testament confirms my quest of Your *words*. I open it at random: "He that hath ears . . . hear." "Hear ye him." So life becomes simply—to hear Your words and do them, moment after moment, one minute at a time. I cannot see far ahead; the details fade as I look far. But that is what faith is for, to keep away worry for the future. "Thy faith hath saved thee" from the future. One minute at a time—this one—listening, saying "Guide my fingers, God, across this page. Guide my thoughts, God, through my brain. Set my love on fire for India's needy multitudes, for the half of the world to whom You have called me." "If ye abide in me." Help me today not to lose the contact even for one minute. My light shines only when the switch is on. Help me not to break this glorious connection, ever.

—— • ——

FRIDAY 15

Calcutta

GOD, how often you speak to us from the pages of the Gospels. "Why do ye not understand my speech?" asks Christ on this morning's page. This morning I seemed to catch a glimpse of the meaning of idols in history, and even today. Sometimes they were used by men who, like myself, fought their own wandering minds in a vain effort not to lose You in the midst of insistent noisy, fascinating distractions. This Testament is a help. A crucifix may help many. A rosary holds the wavering mind. Religious statues and pictures of saints looking heavenward help all of us. An image is useful when it helps us fix the mind fast to God. It is wrong when it makes God small or limited. God *is* in an idol because He is also everywhere. "In hell . . . thou art there."

The escape from idolatry for India is not to stop idolatry, but to help those who worship idols to see God within and beneath all things. Walt Whitman and Wordsworth knew this. So! everything is bathed in God. I swim in God as a fish in the sea. Every object is my idol to remind me of God. So my mind cannot escape! "Thou art there, there, there. . . ."

—— • ——

SATURDAY 16

Asansol

GOD, how wonderfully we do *find* when we *seek*. We find what we seek—and always more! If we seek the best, it is better than we had supposed the best could be. We open doors expecting to find more than we expect. It is always good—plus or bad—plus.

God, help me to welcome each day as a game with circumstances, to conquer the obstacles which rise like fog to shut You out. They call out new strength of will and so develop that strength. Teach me, God, to try hardest when I want to try least. Make me hottest in soul when the environment is coldest, for their sakes who are cold. When in Rome, may I be *unlike* the Romans most!

—— • ——

SUNDAY 17

Buxar V. P., India

GOD, thank You for being my friend when there is no other friend in sight. Thank You for speaking through my voice and telling me that my new life close up to You makes You very happy. So much makes You sad. How my own past must have saddened You. But now Your joy adds to

12

mine. Thank You for the burning axle that led me to stop at Buxar to start the speakers of Bhojpuri toward a new hope. Thank You that when I am sleepy, I can just rest back in trust upon Your breast. I thank You for looking at me through the gentle, dark eyes of that modest Indian girl. Now, for one hour I shall try not to let You escape from my thought for a second.

—— • ——

MONDAY 18

Allahabad

GOD, I have felt Your hand leading today. You have not failed me once in the moments of testing. My job of not forgetting You at all has been imperfect, though better than some other days. Your part of coming to meet my need has been perfect. You, whom we call King, are the most faithful slave of us all, giving air, the sun, food, everything endlessly, love never growing lax. We forget. You never forget, night or day, with the burden of the universe on Your shoulders. At once my King and my Servant, working for and in us, managing our very alimentary canals. I look at a great man or a great cathedral and tremble. Help me to have Your courage.

—— • ——

TUESDAY 19

En route Allahabad
to Jubbulpore

GOD, that group of women weeping as they say farewell to their man reveals the love they hold for him. Are You that love? Are You the love in me this morning that makes me pray for Bob and feel such eager longing to fold the big boy in my arms and help him in his struggles? If You are as I am in Your eagerness for Your children, why does not Your heart break? If I loved these millions as I love Bob, I should go mad with frustrated longings. Even with my weak

13

love I want to weep for them. Yet You, who never sleeps and can never forget one suffering, despairing, fearing, desperate creature for a single second, have the courage to love and suffer the pain of the whole world. You are eternally on Your Cross.

————— • —————

WEDNESDAY 20

Jubbulpore

GOD, this day is packed with important contacts. Speak every word my tongue utters for me. Walk in my mind and think Your thoughts there. Burn in my heart. Direct my eyes. Dwell, love in me all day.

Dwell, too, God, in everyone of us and among us all as we seek Your mind and Your heart concerning literacy and India's need. Set our souls on fire today in this conference so that we may never lose courage again. Not the flare of a sheet of paper—but burn like the eternal sun in our hearts. Then illiteracy will melt away and Christ will rule.

————— • —————

THURSDAY 21

Train Leaving Jubbulpore

GOD, I leave this conference in thanksgiving, believing it was beyond all comparison the best literacy conference we have ever had. Every hour was lived in prayer, and every hour You were present, working to bring Your will to pass, because we gave You a clear channel through which to work. As those delegates go home, God, hold them to their high resolves. You can use my earnest prayer tonight to hold them. So now I pray and will pray tomorrow. Thank you for something inside that aches, God, with intense feeling. It is the way You love India and care for these millions until Your great heart aches!

14

FRIDAY 22

IF continuous communion with You, God, is *possible* for all people under all conditions, it must be possible here in this station with people talking all around me. But it requires a greater effort of the will to concentrate upon You when around me are men who show no evidence of giving You a thought, and when the injustice of master and cringing slave stands out so hideously. God, teach me to love these poor creatures underneath not this moment only. Teach me to have Thine own undying fire and to transmute that fire into a program that will emancipate because it is planned and led by You. As I think down through India, here, God, is a prayer for all who seek Your mind and who long to free slaves.

———— • ————

SATURDAY 23

GOD, thank You for contacts with other earnest souls, for those who poured out the best of life for You when they received little praise from other men. God, as I talked to those new Christians from the depressed classes today, saw their rather dull faces and felt how *far* they seemed to have to go, I could realize a little of all the discouragement You must feel for all of us. But how You must glory in these sacrificial souls who live in tents and try to bring new thoughts of You to the outcastes. God, use my prayer to send them new courage—the world's real heroes! And, O God, take my prayer to help break the deadening indifference and hopelessness of the oppressed millions here.

There Big Ben struck from London over Mr. Lawrence's radio. Was that Your voice, God, from London?

15

SUNDAY 24

HE said, "Where is *your* faith?" We all feel amazed at Jesus and try to give Him *praise*. What God seeks is *not praise*, but *growth* into the likeness of Christ, into the *achievements* of Christ. Any fear that we cannot be like Him, even when we ask God, is what Jesus rebuked and rebukes yet, because we are to *become* strong, not to *apologize* for *failing* all our lives. Astonishment does not please Jesus, for He is not a slight-of-hand performer but fearlessly real. "They being afraid wondered." We do that in the presence of illness or of nature's disasters. We cringe like slaves; we do not stand unafraid like some. In three consecutive pages of Luke, Jesus shows us how to command wind, waves, devils, and death. We are making many Christians in India. We do not seem to be making many *miracle working Christians* like Sadhu Sundar Sing. We preach and practice a *weak* Christianity.

"Be not afraid! Be strong in . . . the power of his might." A flabby Christian too weak to conquer self, afraid of other people—this curses our age.

——— • ———

MONDAY 25

GOD, I thank You for having let me see the Taj Mahal by moonlight, like one of the "many mansions" of heaven descended to earth! Those white fleecy clouds which reached from the fairy dome to heaven were like a net which had just let it down and set it in the moonlight. Perfection in perfect marble! And You are calling us to make such perfection of all this world. No, not *that* perfection built on oppression. But perfection of *love* as harmonious and lovely as the moonlight dream. We begin where we are masters,

16

inside ourselves. We look at Jesus, the Taj Mahal of Spirit. We listen every second while Your still voice directs the building of a Taj Mahal within, built on love—listening and serving.

——— • ———

TUESDAY 26

Agar

GOD, to be under Your will in every act, in every thought —that is my dead-earnest purpose! I grit my teeth tight, for this purpose demands will! I fight to keep my thoughts out of bypaths where You are not leading.

Shall we write a book together about literacy in India? A joint authorship of God and F.L.? The thought came from You this morning, I agree! We will begin to collect our material and lay out our outline when this page is finished. Keep me from doubting or vacillating. Keep me *driving* with You until that work is completed. First, I have this Testament to read. "Her sins, which are many, are forgiven; for she loved much." "Thy sins are forgiven." God, I *do* love much, and so Your words mean me, too.

——— • ———

WEDNESDAY 27

Near Moga

GOD, after a sleepless night, I open my eyes, laughing, for we are together! Sleep is not necessary. Disturbances like that man coughing below me all night are good for character if I do not let them keep me from You. If every annoyance can be made to remind me to turn and grip Your hand and ask You, "What are You saying through this vexation?" then I can turn life's rough spots into Your vocabulary. If I can do that perfectly, nothing can defeat my soul. It will all be on the credit side of the ledger.

"Then welcome each rebuff
That turns earth's smoothness rough."

17

And yet—with the immense task before me—I had no right to lie there permitting myself to be exposed to his cough. I ought to have moved for India's sake.

—— • ——

THURSDAY 28

Lahore [Pakistan]

GOD, unusually lonesome so far as the world is concerned because I am entirely among strangers who are little interested in me and less in my work, I laugh, wholly at ease. This is Your work and You have sent me here. . . .

March, 1937

WEDNESDAY 3

Romans 3   Godhra [India]

GOD, it is very difficult to keep out thoughts which cannot stay in the same mind with Thee. Perhaps that fight, too, is very good for me. Perhaps it is the link of understanding with everybody around me. Sex fancies surge up from the depths of our nature. That is how this morning begins. But I welcome it as a challenge to overcome these enemies of fellowship. I must, I can, I shall overwhelm them today. Here is my will, God, make it triumphant within. If this is possible for people on sick beds, it must be possible for me.

Thus I see that the best gift I have for others is to succeed in this spiritual adventure. "Sail on and on and on!" especially when I do not want to!

——— • ———

THURSDAY 4

Romans 4   En route Allahabad

GOD, I see what is the real curse of our race—so few *do* love their neighbors as themselves. So few *will* sacrifice self-interest to bless all. So few *will* give themselves to the task of aiding 'others. Outside this window I see mile after mile of dry land which would blossom if it had two things— water and freedom from oppressive owners. Sun pumps could be used to draw the water from the earth. But somebody objects that the glass to make sun pumps is expensive. Why expensive? Why could not the immense abundance of sand be used to make this glass in great, cheap quantities? It could, but men do not yet care enough.

19

Or we could teach all India to read if we adopted a simple alphabet. Why do people not do it? Because those who read do not really care for those who are illiterate. It would be so easy, but indifference makes it so impossible.

——•——
FRIDAY 5
Romans 5   Allahabad

GOD, was it my thought of Thee that led the boy in the train to say, "How to find everlasting life is the question." How glad I am that my own personal experience arose to my lips to answer him. What a good illustration of the fact that we need to be full every instant and then just pour out what we have without strain or posing. This morning, as I came from the train and prayed for all the people on the street, I felt new energy surge into me. What it does to all of them to receive that instant prayer I may never know. What it does for me is electrical. It drives out fatigue and thrills one with eager power. How curious one's mind feels thus encircling others. Is Jesus like that?

——•——
SATURDAY 6
Romans 6   Allahabad

GOD, thank Thee for the freshness of discovery, which lends zest to every day, when I listen to Thy voice and wait until Thou leadest. Thank Thee that it has proved right to venture so far on faith. Thank Thee for the way literacy lessons came into being this morning so much better than I had expected. Thank Thee for this splendid group of co-operators who are working so eagerly with me. Thank Thee for the new doors which keep opening for this crusade against illiteracy. Help me, oh, help keep the door open toward Thee and the door closed toward sin in any of its forms. Thine, all Thine, nothing but Thine, walking through the doors Thou dost open, obeying instantly!

SUNDAY 7

Romans 7   **Allahabad**

BEFORE me lies Streeter's *The God Who Speaks*. If Thou dost speak to one, Thou dost speak to all. If Thou dost speak ever, Thou dost speak always. If Thou dost speak anywhere, Thou dost speak everywhere. And I may listen for Thee to speak in the *Bhagavad-Gita*, where we read:

"I am the taste in the water. I am the light in sun and moon, sound in the ether, manhood in men.

"The pure scent in air am I, and the light in fire; the life in all born beings am I.

"I am victory, resolution, the Goodness of those possessed by the Goodness-mood."

Surely Thou canst and dost speak *through* every good for anything may become and does become Thine instrument.

——— • ———

MONDAY 8

Romans 8   **Allahabad**

GOD, thank Thee for yesterday's vision of the Mass Movement. I pray for those men with their white turbans and for those women. God bless that young secretary of the Chamar caste who sought the guidance of Smith. God bless those twenty or more who were baptized. God bless us as we seek to prepare easy ways for them to learn to read.

What a wonderful minute by minute demonstration life is that the one thing needful is to be led by Thee in every decision, in every word.

I felt, God, as if I was fighting confused and clashing thought currents yesterday. Help, God, that all those missionaries may be completely surrendered and not one prove a hindrance, but all prove a great blessing.

21

TUESDAY 9

Romans 9 Allahabad

GOD, thank Thee for the quite wonderful way in which the Hindi and Urdu characters have arranged themselves for learning purposes. It seems a miracle that they should so easily find this arrangement, as though they had been planned for this from eternity. Thank Thee for the way in which my brain works over these ideas and never lets them go until they are perfect. This has surely come from Thee when my windows were open toward Thee. Since I have found by many experiences of the past that new insights were given daily whenever I opened the door to Thee, God, now I am open and eager for fresh revelation.

———— • ————

WEDNESDAY 10

Romans 10 Allahabad

GOD, thank Thee for giving me a new approach this morning as I awoke. It broke upon my consciousness after I had said: "God, Thou knowest the full answer to our question." Then the perfect answer came!

How I do want to succeed in keeping Thee in my thought every second. How I do want to make all thought a process of *consulting* with Thee, for I always get surprises when I am open Theeward and am always barren when I forget Thee. Teach me how to carry everything and every thought to Thee so that at last I will not seek thoughts apart from Thyself, but always take Thee along.

———— • ————

THURSDAY 11

Romans 11 Allahabad

GOD, how marvellously Thou hast broken open this Urdu Dihate set of lessons today. But of all today's miracles, the greatest is this: To know that I find Thee best when I work listening, not when I am still or meditative or even on my

22

knees in prayer, but when I *work* listening and co-operating. Thank Thee, too, that the habit of constant conversation grows easier each day. I really do believe *all* thought can be conversations with Thee. And what is this strange new sense of *knowing answers* instead of being baffled, a sense of intellectual miracles happening. O God, I am so glad to see that our real battles are all in the mind. Outward acts of sin are outcroppings of inner disease. Outward acts of kindness are also outcroppings of fellowship.

—— • ——

FRIDAY 12

Romans 12   Allahabad

GOD, what a wonderful chapter is Romans 12: Be transformed in mind . . . the perfect will of God. . . . Let love be without hypocrisy. . . . condescend to men of low estate. . . . avenge not yourselves. . . . If thine enemy hunger, feed him. . . . overcome evil with good.

Paul has passed over this land I am now exploring.

Weatherhead in his book, *The Transforming Friendship,* finds fellowship with Thee far easier than I find it. He just lets go, believes, and finds it simple. He thinks *will* is not a factor, that resolutions make no difference or at least fail. "Just leave the door to God ajar," he says. Yes, but I have to put the shoulder of my will against that door and keep it open by grim determination. My mind gives me trouble. If Weatherhead had as much sin in his past life as I have had, would it be so easy?

—— • ——

SATURDAY 13

Romans 13   Allahabad

GOD, as I was looking at the food before me and trying to see Thee in it, I lifted it to my lips. Then I realized that I would be eating Thee in that food. Whenever we take any food, Thou art there. I have been seeking to hear Thee and

23

see Thee, but not until now to taste Thee in food, or smell Thee in flowers.

God, help me to keep my head as new, wonderful doors open, like this all-Hindi Revision Committee of the Congress has done.

Dost Thou really suffer from disappointment at our failures? We in this world cannot have the highest type of character unless we suffer for this world. Does the Cross reveal Thy character, God?

—— • ——

SUNDAY 14

Romans 14   Allahabad

GOD, what a wonderful week of work with Thee this good week has been. How marvelously Thou hast kindled my mind to break into new effort. And now, as I am about to leave, here is a prayer for the men who´ are to continue on with experiments. I pray for Ralla Ram, for he knows the secret now, and for all these other loyal persons. Help them to follow the search for Thine answers. As I face this committee on the final revision of the Hindi alphabet, God, accomplish Thy will through me. God, is McGavren right and Miss Chapman and Hivali? Are the Christians the only people Thou desirest to learn to read? I do so want to please Thee. But are not all the people of India Thy children? And if we stop serving them, can we reveal Christ?

—— • ——

MONDAY 15

I Corinthians I   Allahabad

YESTERDAY was to me a series of miracles. The young man who followed me home to tell about his loneliness of soul, the unexpected eagerness of Kaka Kalilkar for a reformed spelling as complete as I was seeking, the eagerness with which he adopted the idea of printing a paper in this simple script, so easy that it could be learned in a day, the couple

24

who asked me to have dinner and who shared with me their spiritual longings—all these things verified my faith. But here, now, is a new day. What fresh miracles will it produce? The *real* question is, "What dost Thou desire done each minute?" I must not worry about surprises but only about perfect, *full* obedience.

—— • ——

TUESDAY 16

I Corinthians 2   **En route to Bombay**

GOD, I thank Thee that the Hindi lessons were completed for the printer. I am glad for the young man who spent an hour sharing his problem about the future. Glad you led me into the Remington offices. Now, God, I face the very important choice of alternatives as to alphabet. Shall I try to introduce my own facial alphabet, or the reformed alphabet which Kaka Kalilkar approved, or labor on with the alphabets now in existence? I am at this extremely important turning of the road. Thou knowest the answer. Give me both faith and the mind *open* heavenward to hear Thy voice so that there may be no regrets. Prepare the leaders of India to accept what Thou dost desire. The utterly simple alphabet seems very hard to promote, but not for Thee, God, is it?

—— • ——

WEDNESDAY 17

I Corinthians 3   **Bombay**

GOD, as I looked at huge Venus, and the inconceivably distant stars, as I gazed through the trees at the awful sun as it set far over the plain, and realized something of its fiery immensity, I remembered that these are mere toys in Thy hands. Thou art everywhere all the time. Then this is my universe too. And when I have done all of this job Thou desirest me to do on earth, I will tackle other jobs with Thee across these mighty reaches. With Thee are an innumerable host of Thy friends. But, God, make my heart tender in

25

eagerness that people all about me in Bombay, in India, in all this world, may share Thee, too. God, should my prayer be more purposive? Are there critical issues that need my prayer at this moment? Does it matter?

——— • ———

THURSDAY 18

I Corinthians 4   **Bombay**

GOD, *more* important than having constant fellowship, is to do Thy desire. Can I tire Thee out with my small chatter as I tired the bishop yesterday? My constant *listening* is Thy desire, and my speaking *only* as Thou dost dictate. What world-need dost Thou desire me to share now in prayer? These depressed classes? Thank Thee for opening the door in this wonderful, unexpected manner to Ambedkar. Yet, what I should do is ask Thee to prepare him and me for the interview. And I do ask Thee for us both, for it may affect all India.

I look at the globe that is set in the picture frame they presented me in Allahabad and pray for Mexico, Camargo, Sanchez, Neff; for Africa and those I am so soon to see there.

——— • ———

FRIDAY 19

I Corinthians 5   **Bombay**

GOD, help that no physical weakness may cause me to fail to do all Thou art planning for today. These new letters came today like an answer, especially from Mrs. Stuhaan who tells of her mystical experiences. We need to cover the world with a mighty network of prayer partners, for it is a big world and the factors opposing Thee are terribly strong.

This is the evening of a lonely, discouraging day. Ambedkar wants the government to do the experimenting, and thinks the new government ought to be approached. Perhaps, but, God—no, this cannot be defeat! This lonely, discouraging day will but help me to sympathize with the millions upon millions upon millions who are discouraged, and will help me to long harder to help and help and help. Some new step has always come out of this kind of discouragement. It will again.

————— • —————

SATURDAY 20

I Corinthians 6   Sholapur

GOD, yesterday I failed to keep close to Thee for hours, and wondered why I could not conquer fever and heat. Today, too, has not been very constant. The tremendous heat is my excuse. But who wants excuses! This, God, is an opportunity to find what obstacles can be overcome. Paul said that nothing can separate us. Can heat? As I try to find improvements for Marathi, God, give me Thy wisdom for their sakes. The lessons must be made easy; in this heat no great effort of the illiterates is possible. Help me, God, to find a way to make it very easy. Thy way, exactly. Thy way, God. *All* Thy way. *Not more* than Thy way, *not less.*

————— • —————

SUNDAY 21, Palm Sunday

I Corinthians 7   Sholapur

AFTER reading in Garland's *Forty Years of Psychic Research* last night, I wonder, God, what immense unseen realities remain to be discovered. But, after all, in all that unseen there are two personalities so infinitely above the rest that I do well to confine my quest to Thee, God, and to Jesus, leaving the others until I step across. But if my grand old father or some others there are helping, and if Thou dost desire me to know it, I am willing. Help me *all day*, all minutes of today, to keep in Thy close presence, to keep listening, on this still Sabbath morning, to Thy voices, all Thy voices from a thousand directions, inner and outer.

27

MONDAY 22

I Corinthians 8   Sholapur

GOD, this discipline of the mind *not* to forget Thee is very, very much the hardest thing I ever tried. I am finding this little globe my best help. It helps me follow Thy thoughts for all men.

This effort must be more than just keeping Thee in mind, something more than constant listening. It must be letting Thee think Thy world thoughts in my mind all day long. Some of those thoughts are close by, some of them far away, wherever the great need happens to be. My thoughts leap to Spain, where hatred has broken loose at its worst. God, I pray for Spain, and I pray that Thy will may be accomplished there. God, can we not find any way to peace and justice? Must justice lie beyond another war? God, I pray for the West. Canst Thou save her from destruction?

——— • ———

TUESDAY 23

I Corinthians 9   Sholapur

LORD, we need more reincarnations of Thy perfect love like the Christ. Is that the goal *every* Christian ought to make his own? The question seems to answer itself. But how, God, can all these little Christians succeed when those who have the best opportunity find it so hard? I see only two things: first, constant outpourings of Thy Holy Spirit; second, the doctrine of ever fresh beginnings. We may forgetfully sink for an hour, but we may also start over at any moment.

But we have not tapped Thy reservoir. That is our real trouble. Thou hast the invisible dust in Thy hands, and not a star or a speck of star dust is out of Thy vision. Thy power to see us through our little problems is limitless. We need only to have connections all the time with Thee.

WEDNESDAY 24

I Corinthians 10   Sholapur

GOD, what marvellous wisdom Paul reveals when he says: "I buffet my body and bring it into bondage." "Let him that thinketh he standeth take heed lest he fall. There hath no temptation taken you but such as man can bear: but God ... will with the temptation make also the way of escape. ... Let no man seek his own, but each his neighbor's good. ... Give no occasion of stumbling, either to Jews, or to Greeks, or to the church of God: even as I also please all men in all things, not seeking mine own profit ... that they may be saved."

What, God, would be for me the highest, utmost possibility for *this minute?* Shall my thoughts enmesh with Thine as Thou dost play over the earth?

———— • ————

THURSDAY 25

I Corinthians 11   Sholapur

GOD, I thank Thee that this new method is attracting so many illiterates and enabling them to teach one another. I thank Thee for the letters from Godhra and Allahabad and Jubbulpore, giving me courage to believe that at last we are on the right track for the languages of India and for students to teach one another. It is Thy gift to India.

Help me not to slump now, but to do *better in keeping close to Thee* than I did the first quarter. This has been far the best three months of my life. I have learned by experience how true it is that I need only *keep close* every minute and Thou wilt do the rest. So, God, may I be closer to Thee and *more constantly* closer.

———— • ————

FRIDAY 26, Good Friday

I Corinthians 12   Poona

JOHN, in chapters 13 through 19, tells about Thursday

night and Friday of the Crucifixion. Alone in this railroad station I hear the echo of that sacred tragedy. Anything I am that is worth being at all, that would be worth perpetuating at all, comes from that sweet sufferer. The moment I allow myself to cut loose from Thee, O Christ of God, I become despicable and my will divides against itself. When my will clings to Thy will, miracles happen. I have seen miracles happening since January. Thou art the vine; this branch and these millions of branches wither except when we abide in Thee. Deeper yet, O Christ, deeper, deeper, yet into Thy broken heart let me bury my will, that from Thy heart I may draw the power of Pentecost. Help me *stay*. Help me *abide*. Nothing else in the world matters but that: the power to stay deep in Thy broken heart.

—— • ——

SATURDAY 27

I Corinthians 13   Bombay

GOD, for the marvellous way Thou didst open up doors in Poona yesterday, I simply sit openmouthed in amazement. For Mr. Bhagwat, that greathearted Brahman; for Mr. Kellock; and Director of Education Grieve, and his fine support. Thou art ahead and will again open all the doors today as Thou dost desire, so that my hopes for Urdu may be realized—our hopes, Father! God, give that other splendid Brahman, Kulkarane in Sholapur, Thy blessing and make him a power. Did I miss an opportunity last night by not listening every moment while with Grieve? Make today a *listening* day, a day of guidance all day.

May I perfectly illustrate in spirit today Paul's marvellous thirteenth chapter of I Corinthians.

—— • ——

SUNDAY 28, Easter Sunday

I Corinthians 14   Bombay

FATHER, just home from Easter morning service. I seem

30

amazed at new discoveries in the world of Spirit. Last night I saw how nearly every person in that church moved, acted as though he saw the vision of Christ, as I tried to help Christ become visible and audible, to help Him plead with each one to give everything, every thought, every minute. Thou art always here. Dost Thou need me to be a medium to help Thee to become visible and audible? The answer seems to be "yes"! Christ, the invisible may be visible, may speak when He can use my mysterious body powers which psychic research seems to prove exist. O Christ, if Thou canst use me, use anything, everything I have!

——— • ———
MONDAY 29
I Corinthians 15   Bombay

GOD, experience proves that a minute *with* Thee *always* brings fruit, often wonderful fruit; experience proves that a minute apart from Thee is wasted or full of thoughts of malice or vice. *Abide* in Me as the branch *abides* in the vine. It *abides all the time,* every moment. Before me is an electric plug. The moment I disconnect the cord, the light goes out. What I got the last minute does not help. I may still be a little warm, but I am no longer a light. "Apart from me ye can do nothing"—say nothing, be nothing, help nothing. So I must *keep plugged* in every second. Hard but essential. Think Thy thoughts, God, here all day—Thine, *not* mine.

——— • ———
TUESDAY 30
I Corinthians 16   Bombay

MY child, this world of the spirit into which you are venturing is as much vaster than the earth you have known, as the fourth dimension is vaster than the third or the third than the second. But beyond the fourth lies the fifth and on on and on. So you must not expect to know the laws of the Spirit until you first face a vast number of facts hard to

31

relate. Those who have seen it and spoken have seen only small fragments. The Apocalypse, Swedenborg, George Fox, Mary Baker Eddy, the spiritualists, the mystics, see in part and do not tell enough to make you able to state the laws of the Unseen. But keep on after discoveries that will exceed anything that hath entered the mind of man.

——— • ———

WEDNESDAY 31

S. S. *Tairea*
Bombay

II Corinthians I

FATHER, there is so much self that obtrudes and makes people unwilling to hear what I have to say about Thee. Perhaps, too, it is my voice or appearance. Perhaps as my wrinkles deepen more people will turn away toward youth. Then nothing can save excepting that Thou wilt fill more and more of the void until at last it is *all* Thyself. Alone on this ship, as the gong tells visitors to leave and as the gangplank descends, help, O help, make these lovely days perfectly Thine. Let us see what can happen to all the passengers if I keep open to Thee and to them the whole long voyage. I leave India with her racial and religious prejudices to enter Africa which is fuller of racial hatred and wrong. O pure Love, possess me as I try to help Africa's tragic millions. (3:00 P.M.)

APRIL, 1937

THURSDAY 1

S. S. *Tairea*

II Corinthians 2   En route to Porbandar

GOD, we can melt away the prejudices and hatred and walls that curse the human race everywhere, only by showing our freedom from these mean little minds. Christ, Thou hast revealed God as love. All over the face of the earth, in every religion, we see other aspects of God. Many are true, and some but partially true, and all too small. The whole universe is too small to reveal more than a minute fraction of God, for infinite time and God only know what fourth, fifth, *n*th dimensions there may be! So, Christ, Thy love should open us all to seek new light from all religions, *not* close us to everybody else as though we already had it all. We have a key—but we *must* use Christ as a key to unlock all truth to all men, not to lock ourselves from people of other faiths.

———•———

FRIDAY 2

II Corinthians 3:3   S. S. *Tairea*

Conscious of God, 25%; Wilful Refusal, None

GOD, for some days, at least, I shall try to give my daily mark on two points, for there have been too many mediocre days this past month. I shall mark first what percentage of the day I was conscious of Thee. Next I shall mark whether my will rebelled against what I believed to be Thy will during the whole day. Perhaps this sense of being marked will keep me at my task.

Then help, Lord, that to *see* anybody will be to pray! To *hear* anybody, as these children talking, that boy crying, may be to *pray!* Help me in this English ship not to expect snob-

bery but friendliness, and when they hold me off, may I
not be sensitive. May I bless the crew, the passengers with
whom I shall work on Gujarati and Kanarese. How would
Jesus act on this ship?

——— • ———

SATURDAY 3

II Corinthians 3   *S. S. Tairea*

Conscious, 50%; Refusal, None

GOD, yesterday was fairly close, yet only about one fourth
of the time was I *conscious* of Thee. Why so small? The
passengers are not religious (excuse number one!). But they
do not know that I am religious. It has not seemed natural
to talk about it to them. Perhaps this is my lesson: To have
God I must give Him at every opportunity. Then the building
of Gujarati charts drew my thought from Thee nearly every
minute. Let me try it today *with* Thee. The preparation of
material for the India report also pushed Thee out. I *did*
remember Thee during much of the ping-pong. Thus far
this morning it has been over 90 per cent. "Ye are . . . an
epistle of Christ . . . written not with ink, but with the Spirit
of the living God." "Ye are . . . known and read of all men."

In this game with minutes we must define our rules: Any
thought of God, Christ, religion, helping others, spiritually
communing with nature, planning a better world, lovingly
talking or praying for others, counts as good if the inner
thought of God comes and goes each minute.

——— • ———

SUNDAY 4

II Corinthians 4   *S. S. Tairea*

Conscious, 75%; Refusal, a Little

GOD, what a marvellous chapter! And three months ago I
would have passed it without comment! "We have . . . re-
nounced the hidden things of shame not walking in craftiness,
nor handling the world of God deceitfully." Just what does this

utterness of surrender mean! And as I see the closing in of physical life, I begin to appreciate II Corinthians 4:7-10. "I believed, and therefore did I speak." God help me to break through this habit of concealment which curses my life.

"Though our outward man is decaying, yet our inward man is renewed day by day. For our light affliction . . . worketh. . . ." Have I not learned that! "We look not at the things which are seen, but at the things which are not seen . . . eternal." One must live to the utmost in order to appreciate Paul. I add *singing prayers* to the list of ways to hold God in mind, or whistling them, or humming them.

————— • —————
MONDAY 5
II Corinthians 5   *S. S. Tairea*
Conscious, 80%; Surrender, Almost Perfect

GOD, it is going to be very difficult to write these percentages truthfully. Somebody may read this diary and call me a weakling. But if, as Paul says, "We must all appear before the judgment seat of Christ," I had better face chagrin now. Paul would say, "You *could* have made yesterday a full 100%." Then why, having started on a *rare* height, did I *will* to read murder tales and "Indiscreet Confessions"? It does seem true that the pendulum, swung beyond normal, swings back. How to prevent that back swing? How to prevent it today all day? I must tackle each minute and be its master, each hour and make it as magnificent as possible. But, God, I am afraid of those grand words. I know too many such words that ended nowhere.

————— • —————
TUESDAY 6
II Corinthians 6   *S. S. Tairea*
Conscious, 25%; Surrender, 50%
"Having nothing, and yet possessing all things. . . . for we

35

are a temple of the living God; even as God had said, I will dwell in them, and walk in them."

When Paul was in the ship en route to Rome, he took possession of it. When Jesus lay asleep in the boat in Galilee, He awoke to take possession of it. As I learn all the possibilities of life, I shall take possession of the ships on which I ride. I shall not again ride in a ship and let circumstances rule me. God dwelling in me. I shall make circumstances do His full will. I shall *find* a way through defenses which people throw around themselves. I shall try to the *full* to find what prayer can accomplish while talking and playing with people. Help me keep this purpose *fixed*.

———— • ————

WEDNESDAY 7

II Corinthians 7   S. S. *Tairea*
Conscious, 75%; Surrender, 100%

AS I sat devoutly at the morning mass yesterday, I wondered whether the wise, old Roman Catholic Church did not perhaps work a real miracle at the Eucharist after all. Do they help Thee, Christ, to materialize for some of those present? Does faith make it possible for Thee to be present, and canst Thou thus make Thyself more real to the worshipers because of a full church? And does the semidarkness with candles prove a better environment than a bright light would be?

Yesterday, Lord, I saw how an experiment in prayer may be tried by athletes! I tried to put my arm in Thy control and my playing improved so much that instead of losing, I won. I tried to put my opponents arm under Thy control and believe he did better. We humans have not begun to suspect what a field for useful scientific research prayer is!

36

THURSDAY 8

II Corinthians 8   *S. S. Tairea*

Conscious, 75%; Surrender, 100%

GOD, last night we crossed the equator. We saw nothing, felt nothing, save the laughter of merrymakers. Yet the equator is a fact in Thy mind and in our minds. And I begged Thee to help me cross an equator of the soul, out of weakness into integration and constant strength, to make this day and the future 100% days in surrender. All of them!

God, that crimson, blood-smeared sunset over Africa was Thy call, and I listened to it for half an hour. Africa needs us. God, we have a key to Christ, to hope, to justice. O God, I fear my weak self! Do not let me ever lose that glorious vision!

Thou, Lord, dost talk, and art talking now! This beautiful "Salutation of the Dawn" is Thy eager voice. "Look to *this* day, for it is life. Today well lived makes every yesterday a dream of happiness. . . ." How happy yesterday leaves me this morning! And an ancient Sanskrit writer knew that!

——— • ———

FRIDAY 9

II Corinthians 9   *S. S. Tairea*

GOD is opening doors! This good Bishop who read the International Review of Missions article and told me he strongly backed me. He said that Africa has a hundred million less people than formerly, that forced labor was the reason, and that he would speak with the Fathers at Mombasa and see what could be done. What can be done? What can be done for the darkest, bloodiest, saddest spot in all the world, so near Abyssinia where six thousand more were massacred a few days ago? My stomach is sick, my heart breaks, I cannot see through these tears. O spirit of Livingstone, can I help the land you opened and where you perished? This

37

Colonel said, "The Africans are the most gentlemanly, courteous, likeable men on earth." And we whites are often beasts! God, help me to help Julia Kellersberger and all other burning hearts to help Thee help helpless Africa.

—— • ——

SATURDAY 10

II Corinthians 10

Train to Nairobi
Kenya [Africa]

GOD, on this immense and almost uninhabited plain will one day dwell millions of happy people, in a world where they will know how to treat one another like brothers. Will this color line persist? Or will we plan for the children who are to come regardless of their color, realizing that we must not only serve men today but also serve the unborn. Would not the idea of planned babies be in line with the spirit of Jesus? Does it make any difference, after all, what color of skin the heirs of the earth possess? To be even a little like Thee, it is necessary not only to think of the whole world but also of the future, to plan for tomorrow, to dream with H. G. Wells of the perfect world that is to come, and we help Thee bring it into Africa. Here is a marvellous opening for lovers of men.

—— • ——

SUNDAY 11

II Corinthians 11

Jeanes School,
Nairobi

GOD, I love these Africans, with their friendly, happy dispositions and their willingness to help! What a contrast to the selfishness one finds on the trains in India! How much freer from snobbery than whites! As Thou art looking down upon this human family, if Thou wert to whisper in my ear the people Thou lovest *most,* would they be the blacks? No, for skins are not black nor white to Thee, races are not races to Thee. Nor dost Thou love men for what they *are,* but rather for that vision of what they *can be* and *will* be when they surrender and allow miracles to happen minute by minute. Help, God, that today I may take the whole roof off my soul and let Thee pack every corner with love every minute of today. Then I shall fit into Thy plan for Africa. Eyes, fingers, tongue, thoughts guided by the Voice of Silence.

——— • ———

MONDAY 12

II Corinthians 12   Kenya
En route to Kisumu

GOD, these primitive faces, people clothed in rags, and low grass huts of the stone age, surrounded by British homes crowd time's awful reach into the same hour. Those dirty clothes full of holes are so like the parts of civilization these people get—its dirt, and its rags, the tatters of our civilization.

I hope that a thousand years hence people will look back and see how primitive our souls are. Our Mussolinis, our hypocritical rich, pretending to believe in Christ! We have just passed a lovely home established by some Englishman, with a delightful green arbor. Is that his contribution to Africa? Then with me is Archdeacon Owen giving himself for Africa—is his gift not the realer?

God, how the women of the world need light! especially these Kikuyu women with their distorted ears and their painful burdens.

——— • ———

TUESDAY 13

II Corinthians 13   Kisumu
Lake Victoria, Kenya

LORD, will Lake Victoria, with this thirty-mile-wide plain, one day be the site of a mighty civilization? What frightful crimes have stained these shores—and all shores where men have ever lived—the veil of the past may conceal. But, God, how canst Thou and I actively, purposefully help those who are consciously or unconsciously preparing the way for to-morrow? Can soul-force help Thee and these Africans about the Lake? Wilt Thou dream Thy dreams *with* and *in* me for this continent? The British government seems to be doing better than I had hoped. Direct my act and thought so that all Thy will may come to pass tomorrow or tonight. My soul goes out to the Kellersbergers as they pray and toil for Christ in the Congo. May my fire re-enkindle their fire.

——— • ———

WEDNESDAY 14

Galatians 1   Kisumu Hotel
                                                     Lake Victoria, Kenya

GOD, thank Thee for the violin and piano music which took hold of me with resistless power and demanded that I should come back to a new level. Thank Thee for the sense of power that swept like a wave around the guests in this hotel, for the purpose to help all of them, for the grip of Thy plan for the future of Lake Victoria. May the imprint of this purpose drive deep into the hearts of us all. Thou hast spoken straight out of the unseen to us all and across all Africa and around the whole world. Thank Thee for the power to help Thee ride into the secret places of men's hearts on the wings of music, for the *tremendous* power of silent self-giving. God, how can we weak things keep on *this* plane?

——— • ———

THURSDAY 15

Galatians 2   Maseno, Lake Victoria
                                                                    Kenya

GOD, what a future *can* belong to these magnificent black Dhuluo boys and the others in this school! How reverent they were! What power in that deep-toned "Amen" from 150 throats!

Back in their homes, their mothers and fathers are ignorant

40

but eager to learn. Help us tomorrow to find a way so that this campaign may sweep like an epidemic through all Africa, a beneficent epidemic of release and hope, and the smile of Christ!

And now, God, as we undertake this first African language, have Thy perfect way, so that we may go straight and true to Thy will. We do our best and highest for Africa only if Thou art the author and finisher. I yield all—fingers, thoughts, love, lips—to Thee.

——— • ———

FRIDAY 16

Galatians 3   Maseno, Lake Victoria
                                                           Kenya

GOD, I have found by unhappy experiences that unless I talk to others about this experiment, my day is a failure. Is that a law of this spiritual adventure? If I do not set the pace, if I do not create the atmosphere, I become a mere victim of conditions. My environment makes me, but I choose the environment. This Testament, this "Fellowship of Silence," this "Great Souls at Prayer," this "Devotional Diary," this book "Awake"—these are my morning teachers because I attend their school. And this "Fourfold Sacrament" is like a gentle angel hand across my brow, like the soft notes of a faint violin, like the heartaches of those who love. This "Sacrament of Work" is Thee speaking.

Lord, teach us to love,

Teach us to love in perfection,

Obeying Thine own great command

That we love one another even as Christ loved us.

Thank Thee, Father, for this morning which leaves me feeling melted all over with Christ-love.

41

Galatians 4

Maseno

Lake Victoria

GOD, thank Thee for St. Patrick's Lorica, or hymn, speaking across thirteen centuries:

"I arise today
Through God's strength to pilot me:
God's might to uphold me,
God's wisdom to guide me,
God's eye to look before me,
God's ear to hear me,
God's word to speak for me,
God's hand to guard me. . . .

* * * * * * * * * * * *

"Christ with me, Christ before me, Christ behind me,
Christ in me, Christ beneath me, Christ above me,
Christ on my right, Christ on my left,
Christ when I lie down, Christ when I sit down,
                    Christ when I arise.
Christ in the heart of every man who thinks of me,
Christ in the mouth of every one who speaks of me,
Christ in every eye that sees me,
Christ in every ear that hears me.

"I arise today
Through a mighty strength, the invocation of the Trinity."

———•———

SUNDAY 18

Galatians 5

Maseno

"THE fruit of the Spirit is love, joy, peace, longsuffering, gentleness, goodness, faith, meekness, temperance." Paul speaks of "Faith which worketh by love." He says, ". . . by love serve one another."

"Father,
Dear Father,
My soul reaches up once more to Thee,
For Thy morning Kiss.
Because Thou, Father God, art Ruler and Lover in one."

What use of this day will wreathe Thy lips with happy smiles, Father, and make Thee give me a kiss of good night with the words, "Well done"? *How* loving, *how* large must my thought be? Only one simple task—to keep the window wide open, to *try* to keep consciously obedient to Thy voice— and Thou wilt tell all the rest.

—— • ——

MONDAY 19

Galatians 6   Kima
                                                Lake Victoria, Kenya

THANK Thee, Father, for the wonderful committee that pushed these lessons today. For women like Mrs. Ludwig and Mrs. Hull to throw their whole souls into preparing pictures.

As the radio in the next room reaches across to England and all the world, so let our prayers for the world reach around to every part of the world. What new era are the radio and the airplane and perhaps television ushering in? Is this the day when walls between nations will crumble and a world brotherhood will begin? God, where are those who are ready to join Thee and one another in drawing men into a loving, united brotherhood?

—— • ——

TUESDAY 20

Ephesians 1   Kima

Among these real, practical, unpretentious people my heart *longs* to be real. May I not try to be superior but to be simple and dependable and honest. Here the rawest of raw material is being brought into touch with Christ.

43

Thank Thee for the gratitude of these fine folk, for the excellent progress our lessons made, for the miracle that sent me *here* where they need and want my help. My heart thrills at beholding Thy hand ever over the horizon. It *was* Thy hand that sent me into the heart of Africa, and wonderful results will burst upon this country. God, speak comfort to the lonely heart of this missionary who buried wife and three babes here.

—— • ——

WEDNESDAY 21

Ephesians 2   **Kisumu**
                                                 Lake Victoria

FOR the first time this year, God, I have been compelled to write this diary a day late. But it is far better to have lived as I have lately than to write about living. What utterness of consecration, what simplicity, what love of the Negroes, what practical common sense, in this mission of the church of God! For the chapel crowded with black faces hiding Thy children, for their music, for putting the right message on my lips—Father, thank Thee.

God, for all the millions of mind-darkened people around this great lake basin, I pray. For these Bunyore people and these Dhuluo people for whom we made language lessons, I pray. For the missionaries, for their co-operation, I pray, that "they may be one."

—— • ——

THURSDAY 22

Ephesians 3   **En route from Kisumu**

GOD, to build the new habit in my mind requires a gentle and nearly constant pressure of the will. Teach me to apply this pressure more continuously and with more effectiveness in praying for others, for Thou dost desire us to be *powerful* as well as clean. "That ye may be strengthened with *power* through his Spirit in the inward man"—power to see souls

44

behind faces, power to pray for those I see outside this car window, power to ooze into or push into the inner souls of others with my prayer and carry Thee with me all the way to the center. Last night, as I prayed hard for those Kima students, I felt that they felt that outreach. Does some emulation reach people? I not only dare, I *must* find out, now that this possible channel of working for Christ has revealed itself. *"Power* through his spirit." Help me not to look at these half-naked savages as curiosities but with eager desire to help Thee reach them.

——— • ———

FRIDAY 23

Ephesians 4   En route to Kikuyu

GOD, what stupendous conceptions are packed in Paul's letter! What a soul Paul had, what penetration into this world of Spirit which I begin to explore! Only one was ahead of him as he passed on into the land no human being had ever before explored. "The mystery, which for all ages hath been hid in God." "Christ Jesus . . . in whom we have boldness and access in confidence." Paul, daring to go on alone, away from the childhood in which all men were, and nearly all men still are—pressing on "unto a fullgrown man, unto the measure of the stature of the fulness of Christ." "For the perfecting of the saints. . . ." ". . . be renewed in the spirit of your mind, and put on the new man. . . . Let all bitterness and wrath, and anger, and clamor, and railing be put away from you, be ye kind one to another, tenderhearted, forgiving each other, even as God also in Christ forgave you." That sick little Jew with that Titan soul!

——— • ———

SATURDAY 24

Ephesians 5   Kikuyu

GOD, how like a game life is! Why not call it a game with minutes? Under all sorts of handicaps which must be faced

45

and overcome, I have one goal to reach, filling that minute with useful fellowship with Thee, and with service directed by Thee. This morning, with eyes aching, my game is to win through as though there were no handicaps.

Thank Thee for those sleepless hours which I used to try to send the picture of Christ to people near and far around the world. I must *grow* in this *power* to help others to contact with Thee, and such growth will come only from exercise. Thou dost need us to be *effective* as well as devoted.

——— • ———

SUNDAY 25

Ephesians 6   Alliance School
                                                Kikuyu

GOD, thank Thee for making the *gentle pressure of the will* change this morning's atmosphere, so that a church service changed from cold to warm. I must learn that *will* and *thought* can change the world, and I must teach other Christians to use that mighty, gentle power.

An idea that the sun pump will some day be a boon to the human race takes hold of me. Is it a vision I share with Thee? If it is, then give me perseverance to see it through.

Thank Thee for the mind-bent that broke into an empty conversation today and made it of permanent value to us all. Thank Thee for this wonderful letter from a prayer partner.

Four things are immensely right: Prayer every minute, prayer for others, this prayer partnership, this literacy effort.

——— • ———

MONDAY 26

Philippians 1   Kikuyu

"LET your life be worthy of Christ, with one soul striving for the faith." This living on the highest plane is a matter of constant choice of the highest thing to think or see or do at each moment. Often when I turn toward the *highest* my brain is blank. Then I can say, "Father I am empty,

46

waiting to be filled, listening for Thee to speak." Nothing is higher than listening to God, unless it be suffering with others and for others. To go through a black hospital without suffering acutely is an indication of low sympathy and lack of love. Measure your Christlikeness by your capacity to share other people's pain and to have an overwhelming desire to relieve.

——— • ———

TUESDAY 27
Philippians 2   Alliance School
                                                 Kikuyu

MY child, when you pray to Me of your own little troubles and doubts, your prayer is pretty thin and small. When you reach out to help other people by offering yourself as a channel for Me, your prayer becomes at once large and noble. You need not pray about your own personal affairs at all, for I will provide for those. Pray for others! Make your whole day a prayer for others. Think of them one by one, and try to help them to a rich contact with Me. Your effort to bring the picture of Christ into their minds was good. I will day by day teach you endless ways to make this priceless voyage of discovery in a little-known land of the Spirit. Put a gentle but continuous pressure on your will to do this. When reading, put your will effort into those of whom you read. When talking, pour your prayer into those to whom you speak and of whom you speak. Thus you will learn what Christ-love in all its fullness and irresistable power is, a terrific, outreaching love-will.

——— • ———

WEDNESDAY 28
Philippians 3   Alliance School
                                                 Kikuyu

"NOT that I had already obtained or am already made perfect . . . but one thing I do, forgetting the things which

47

are behind, and stretching forward . . . I press toward the goal . . . the high calling of God in Christ Jesus." Was it the high price Paul paid or pain he endured that whipped up his passion for Christ? Can any man conquer the dulling effect of comfort?

Last night I saw one new advance in this experiment with Thee. I saw that the best way to pray for others is to say: "Christ show me where Thou art seeking entrance in vain so that I may add my prayer and help Thee enter." The faces floated before my eyes. Thank Thee when sleepless hours come that give me time to pray for many.

Thank Thee for the soul hunger in the missionaries here, the soul hunger which came to meet mine at last night's meeting. This is new evidence that this road will help other Christians.

——— • ———

THURSDAY 29

Philippians 4   Alliance School
                                                         Kikuyu

MY son, I have seen races slowly emerge from savagery to some degree of kindliness as centuries rolled by. England is better now than in the fierce days of the invaders. And I can wait while out of this racial wrong some better race emerges in Africa. I wait, but this betterment does not happen by accident. I wait for men and women who will surrender their lives wholly and eagerly, who will ache with eager longing to bless Africa, who will be consuming fires, zealously self-giving. There *are* such men and women now, and each one pushes Africa upward toward her better day.

"But what of the millions who have lived and are living with no opportunity to know the higher life?" you are asking. If you learn to *see* just around you, you will know that *life* stretches on and on, with ample ages in which to fulfill what these brief days lack. All of you are but gurgling infants as yet, all of you.

———— • ————

FRIDAY 30

Colossians 1   Alliance School
                                                Kikuyu

TODAY, Father, closes the four most glorious months of my life. With what conviction of experience I can now *urge* youth to try to have glorious years! As I look back over this uneven life, there is much I want to hide forever in the crimson flood of Christ's blood. But the high years are sources of joy: The year when Tommy Ash led me to the Methodist altar; the year in Perkiomen; the year in Spring Street; the years when I wandered over America speaking; the first year in Lanao [Philippines]; last year in America; but far above them all these four months! We are stepping into a new world hand in hand, and sailing with thrilling eagerness toward unknown shores.

Not where one is is most significant, but the direction and speed with which one is *going*. I *know* that the best gift I have for the world is to help men discover this new continent of the Spirit, to discover it for them and beckon them to come.

At fifty-two nothing I ever did is worth preserving except the high aspirations. They are my "treasures in heaven." God, help me to continue that gentle but incessant pressure of the will "on and on and on"!

49

May, 1937

SATURDAY 1

Colossians 2   En route Nairobi to Mombasa

GOD, two lessons came out of this day. Last night, because my hosts served sherry, I assumed they would not be interested in the realm of the spirit. Then I saw in their library Nikolai Berdiaev's *Freedom and the Spirit,* and today told them a little. "How perfectly thrilling!" exclaimed one of them. Lesson 1: I must hide what I have from *nobody.*

These grand people, Mr., Mrs., and Miss Grieve, to whom I told all during my week with them, came all the way to Nairobi to see me off, and by their looks and words proved (Lesson 2) that friendship is far, far best when we share our deepest highest best selves with one another. I cannot forget the hand grips of others who attended the Tuesday night prayer meeting, and said they could never express their gratitude. God, help me to love to share with strangers.

————— • —————

SUNDAY 2

Colossians 3   In front of a Barroom
Mombasa

GOD, how strange to be writing *this* in a town where I have no friends, in a hotel outside the barroom window, Sunday morning, and not to feel alone, "For thou art with me." I try to see Thy sweet face on this chair in front of me. I try to help Thee step into the mind of the chauffeur in that car; and he turns to look, as nearly all people do now. So here I am *manufacturing* my atmosphere with nothing but my Testament and this diary to help me help Thee change my

50

environment. We must be masters in every situation in order to win this constant war. I am amazed at the way that chauffeur glues his eyes on me, and the bartender comes out to look. *Here* and in places like this are where Christ needs help most. The Salvation Army is tremendously right. The rest of us confuse fastidious snobbery with religion and become Pharisees, thanking God that we are not as that bartender. So we say we "fight" sin by avoiding sinners, while Jesus was a friend of sinners and ate with them. He sought incessantly to help *others;* we seek merely to save *ourselves.*

——— • ———

MONDAY 3

Colossians 4   *S. S. Chantilly*
                                    Mombasa to Zanzibar

"PERFECT and complete in all the will of God." "Continue steadfastly in prayer, . . . praying for us also, that God may open unto us a door for the word, to speak the mystery of Christ."

Another even more strange situation today is the one on this French ship. Almost all passengers are unable to speak English, and I speak such poor French that they would dislike talking with me. A perfect chance to try what sheer, steadfast prayer can do! So I will today try to help Thee reach into the heart of each passenger I meet. Can we make a real advance in this prayer art today? There are two things with which we deal—power to press through and pure quality of our message when we do get through. The latter is something Thou only canst give. So my simple task is to *listen* and *follow.* The channel is wide open from Thee to them all day long! Come, Spirit, and rush through and out like a reversed waterspout! Downward and outward. . . .

51

TUESDAY 4

I Thessalonians I   Zanzibar
                                    English Club House

GOD, the laboratory of each day's experience teaches two
lessons and proves them valid. First, when a man is speaking with me, pouring out his long story, he has *opened* his
mind to me, he is tuned in; and while I listen I can be sending back to his mind my silent prayers for God to enter. All
over the world are people anxious to talk to us. Let them
tell it! and call it God's opportunity. Second, I am like an
oarsman rowing against a current. My *will-pressure must be
gentle but constant,* to listen to God, to pray for others incessantly, to look at people as *souls* and not as clothes, or
bodies, or even minds. The moment the pressure on the oar
ceases, I drift, and downward. . . . "Let go and let God" does
not fit my experience. "Take hold and keep hold of God" is
what it feels like to me. There is a *will-act,* and I can feel
the spiritual muscles growing from rowing!

————— • —————
WEDNESDAY 5

I Thessalonians 2   Zanzibar

GOD, Thou dost never fail us. This morning I listened and
prayed, while this committee did the work, and Thou didst
guide us. What resulted must have seemed like magic to that
committee. It did also to me!

As I reread those glorious letters from my prayer regiment,
I realized that we make our own heaven! We build it, and
then inhabit it. Rather, we plant it like a mustard seed; and
Thou givest the crop. I planted ideas which came from Thee,
and all these people have given the good thoughts back with
interest. Why must one wait until he is fifty-two to learn that
what a man sows he shall reap? Why cannot youth know
that without first sowing hell?

52

THURSDAY 6

I Thessalonians 3   Zanzibar

SURE as life, God, Thou art at work! Daily I see Thy
hand! Out from the library shelves stood *Raymond* by Oliver
Lodge, *Human Personality* by F. W. H. Myers, *The Vital
Message* of Conan Doyle, and Barrett's *On The Threshold
of the Unseen*. My voyage of spiritual discovery must not
ignore those amazing findings.

But they are not to deflect me from my course, which is
straight toward Thee. They may encourage and suggest but
not retard or confuse. *It is simple* now, when my *will* must
simply be pressed toward Thee, endlessly and gently toward
Thee!

And this wonderful third chapter of Thessalonians is Thy
voice. It contains a *mighty* will, a *mighty* love, a *mighty*
loyalty, and *mighty* courage in persecution.

——— • ———
FRIDAY 7

I Thessalonians 4   Zanzibar

GOD, I stand today on the edge of another form of in-
tercessory prayer and hesitate whether to follow a path so
unusual. Last night, when wakeful, I closed my eyes in the
darkness and took a journey with my mind to some of my
friends, imagined myself walking into their homes, shaking
hands and then saying, "I have come to say: The Spirit of
Jesus floods your minds and your hearts." Then I said farewell and came back to Zanzibar. Is it *right?* If it helps people
to a fuller experience of Christ, it is *necessary* as well as right
to use any door God opens. Is this the new experience Thou
hast opened through Lodge and Barrett? I must try before
I know whether it is fruitful and really reaches others. I will
begin systematically with a notebook.

GOD, You *do* step out of the pages of books into our minds! What a succession of wonderful visions You gave me just now from this letter of Paul's! His words shoot into me like bullets, every sentence a bull's-eye.

You *are* speaking from the pages of Sir Oliver Lodge, "Christ was a planetary manifestation of Deity, the highest and simplest to man, a revelation in the only form accessible to man, a revelation in the full-bodied form of humanity." Jesus enables us to trust God—God's pity, His love, His friend liness, His compassion, His eager desire to help men—so that in Christ I need fear neither man nor devil nor death itself. *Death*—a new adventurous voyage of discovery.

But, God, You do not step forth from books unless we seek books where You are to be found. The detective story I read yesterday was a sheer waste of time.

——— • ———

SUNDAY 9

GOD, to whom I write on this page, is there any truth in the words of this Sana-Veda? "If thou sayest, 'I know Him in part,' thou deceivest thyself, for not to be wholly ignorant of Him is not to know Him. He who believes that he does not know Him is he that does know Him."

My child, this is both true and false. They who believe they finally know My secret are very foolish. They who, like the materialists of your day, make silly little denials about Me are caught in pure ignorance and will appear as ridiculous to men a century hence as Butler does to you now.

But, though you cannot know *all* while on that plane, you can speak and I will hear, you can hear and I will speak, you can follow and I will lead, you can obey and I will direct. But if you refuse, My heart aches, for I know how yours must ache before you return to Me. You are crossing the stage of eternity as I venture upon an experiment in free wills, and those who prove that I can trust them with Sonship shall one day know all.

—— • ——
MONDAY 10

II Thessalonians 1   Zanzibar

GOD, I seem to be discovering with dizzy speed how *wide* this spiritual Universe may prove to be. Thou art placing before me books which exceed all I had dreamed I might see. Maeterlinck's *The Great Secret* collects with convincing power the new scientific evidence of the spiritual world. Then these three volumes of Swedenborg, *Heaven and Hell, The Divine Love and Wisdom, The Divine Providence,* seem to be saying exactly what these modern books seem to tell of the unseen, though Swedenborg lived two centuries ago. Help me with unbiased, fearless mind to *"weigh and consider"* evidence from *whatever source,* for, like my race and age, I have been dogmatic, narrow, and proud of my blindness. What a little man, in what a big universe! How sure on what meager evidence! Teach me to be open-minded and quietly humble—but burning up with passion to help others!

—— • ——
TUESDAY 11

II Thessalonians 2, 3   Zanzibar

OVERWHELMED by the sense of Thy stupendously immense power and size and wisdom, as these books truthfully remind me, and of my own stupid, blundering, frail little soul and body, I am ashamed of the way I have so often approached Thee. Why are we so *weak,* why these clouds in our *memories* and *thoughts?* But then I hear You reply:

"My little one, I never felt hurt at your familiar way of coming to Me. It is *neglect* that grieves Me, because you cut

55

yourself off from wisdom and love. I want you to be at perfect ease anywhere, through your trust in Me.

"But as for weakness, you mortals have all the powers I dare give you. See what Western men do with chemistry! Suppose I gave you the secret of atomic energy now. I must permit the far more worthy secrets of the soul to be known to a few—the rest would use them to ruin the world. So telepathy is guarded by love, and only they who love can use it."

—— • ——

WEDNESDAY 12
Coronation of George VI
I Timothy I ·   Residency, Zanzibar

GOD, as the British Empire crowns its new king today, what a surging of varied and often disharmonious emotions pulsate in millions of breasts. Thank Thee for the mighty emotions and the sense of world vision Thou gavest me during that service this morning, when my thought reached out and gripped this floating ball called earth and I willed unity, love, Christ for every nation and color. Did all the people in that church, did all the British Empire, did all the world feel that vibration? Now while the British Isles are alive with the great day, I sit here and try to help Thee reach through this excitement to men's hearts. Use me to change Mussolini! Use me to reach Spain. Use me to reach Hitler and set him right! Shall I journey to them in thought and try to talk to them for Thee? I *will try!* (12:00 noon)

—— • ——

THURSDAY 13
I Timothy 2   Zanzibar

GOD, if Jesus sat here permitting Thee to write, what wouldst Thou say? What dost Thou desire done today? Thank Thee for permitting me to share in opening the new door through Mrs. Johnson's Moslem Girls school. Thank

Thee that they needed an interpreter, because I had a chance to pray after each sentence. Thank Thee for the incredible way in which doors have flung open here for Hindus, Arabs, Africans. For those three hundred who came last night, show me how *most* effectively to pray for them, and for the women in that girls school, and for the Indian teachers, and the African teachers. I shall try to listen carefully so that Thou canst reveal the *best* possible method of teaching Swahili. Thank Thee for new vistas I just begin to see. May all Thy will, all Thy love—work today, all the minutes.

——— • ———

FRIDAY 14

I Timothy 3   En route to Dar es Salaam

GOD, for this privilege of sharing the dreams of a young doctor and planning for a better world, I thank Thee. Help me, God, to become freer from boasting about America and to feel only for Thee each minute. I often slump so badly below the ideal when in conversation with others, and talk too much, not waiting until Thou hast said Thy mind. Was this list of world needs *Thy* list of needs: co-operative societies, planetary mindedness, openness toward the Spirit, the zest for discovery in every important direction—was that enough?

My thought returns to that committee of Arabs who responded so wonderfully this morning. I think ahead to Dar es Salaam, and want *all, all, all* Thy will, *only* Thy will done while there. *All, only.*

——— • ———

SATURDAY 15

New Africa Hotel
Dar es Salaam

GOD, our silver wedding day and ten thousand miles apart. If this had been two years ago, how desperately lonely I

57

should have felt. But Effa and I are not apart. I can send my soul to her and she hers to me. Soul is all that has permanent significance. And Thou art *working through* me this morning. My soul has stepped forth to bear Thy picture, Christ, Thy love-will to all the people in this hotel, to all the voices I heard outside, to scores who floated into my memory across the globe. And I am astonished to find that there is not a trace of loneliness this morning; space does not exist for the soul that knows how to leap and reach! Tongue and pen become secondary, for thoughts fly anywhere with more than light's swiftness. The world belongs only to those who hold it in their arms and pray for it. Government titles are delusions.

——— • ———

SUNDAY 16

I Timothy 4   Dar es Salaam
                                                               Hotel

GOD, in this voyage of discovery in the world of Spirit some amazing surprise awaits around nearly every corner. "The laying on of hands" really *does* something if it be true that our souls are radioactive. There is truth in the Roman Catholic doctrine of apostolic succession. The Roman Catholics are wrong when they say theirs is the only succession— as negatives are more often false than true.

From now onward I shall search for some secret wrapped in every superstition and in every religion that grips men's hearts. They meet or offer to meet some human need. Paul might have meant me instead of Timothy when he said, "Meditate upon these things; give thyself wholly to them; that thy profiting may appear to all." "Be thou an example of the believers." *Wholly*—that is what I need more of Thy help to achieve. In the tired hours of the afternoon "our souls grow weary." Help this day to be *wholly* at its best

58

conquering this hotel atmosphere—wholly! Make me ready for miracles today!

———— • ————

MONDAY 17

I Timothy 5   Dar es Salaam
                                      The Dar es Salaam Club

GOD, a great many pious thoughts protrude from my consciousness like rocks sticking out of the ocean, but they are not the *highest*, the last *highest*, are they? They are not the thoughts in Thy mind. May I ask Thee to think in my mind?

"To grant that *fully*, My child, would be for you to think all My infinitely countless thoughts at once. You are not safe for that, are you? The universe would be in peril if you possessed that much power before your *will* is *perfect*. And when your *will* becomes *perfect*, you will ask Me that all these Africans, all these Europeans may also share all My thoughts. You will not ask more for yourself than you do for everybody. And you are far from that in your daily practice."

God, save me from being dragged even further toward unconscious snobbery by the luxuries of this club and the attentions of officials. Do *something* to save me for everybody. Thou hast done it, for even now I can reach the arms of my soul around every soul in the world!

———— • ————

TUESDAY 18

I Timothy 6   Dar es Salaam Club

MARVELOUSLY close, God, help me to keep thinking of Thee all day today, as love crowding gently as the ether, warm as the sunlight, into every nook and cranny of my thoughts, words, looks, acts—love pressing in, and oozing out, floating like perfume out to others.

59

"O Love that wilt not let me go,
I rest my weary soul in Thee;
I give thee back the life I owe,
That in Thine ocean depths its flow
May richer, fuller be."

"My child, this makes Me happy. Now let love flow out
to My world of needy people all about you. Despise not one
of the least. Do not see color or clothes, just souls and My
children. Do not hear titles or languages, just hear Me speak
through them. I call from behind every eye, I float upon
every wave of speech and song and sigh. See Me in people,
for I seek to make them grow in Christlike love."

———— • ————

WEDNESDAY 19

II Timothy I   Dar es Salaam

FATHER, here is my willing hand to be directed across
the page by Thee. Here is my brain; walk through it and
put its thoughts in order after Thine own love-will. I wait
unwilling to write save as I am sure Thou art directing.

"My child, hold up to this high effort all day long. As
you reached upward and outward yesterday morning and
evening, learn habitually to keep that outreach for everybody whom you meet or think of every minute. Do not
surrender to your tired feelings, for this outreach-upreach
does not exhaust you. It can be the constant state of mind. Yes,
you may read the books written on clairvoyance and witch-
craft, but not much, for your fellowship with Me directly
is the pearl of great price. So saturate your spirit in Me."

———— • ————

THURSDAY 20

II Timothy 2   Dar es Salaam

GOD, my education is only just beginning this year. Indeed, it may not advance far in this life. We humans stand

on the edge of a vast unknown and are wise only when we realize how little we know, as *Ether and Reality* by Oliver Lodge reminds us. We may spend eternity learning. . . .

This couple, Mr. and Mrs. Dowd, who were married today at such a mature age will need Thee, Lord. Did they not need me and did I not fail them? I should have *found* a chance to help them. Help me, God, to press *every last drop out of each opportunity to help people,* and not to yield to the habit of running away from people. Make me always sensitive to the need of others, keen to sense the carefully hidden need!

I will pray for them now, 9:30 P.M.

Father, Thou art planning and working. Thank Thee for the success of the Swahili charts today, astonishing all of us.

——— • ———
FRIDAY 21
II Timothy 3   Dar es Salaam

DEAR, dear Father God, pour in and through and out over the world; begin this early hour and continue until these eyes close in sleep after a glorious day of serving as Thy roadway into men's souls. I almost gasped at the amazing wisdom packed into this third chapter of Timothy and at the *power* with which it set my own soul electric! Are these words of Aldous Huxley true or false: "The perfect height cannot be lived on, only visited—the soul cannot always feel what it feels sometimes—ecstatic states are rare—man has one hour of ecstasy in every hundred." Perhaps true of him and those he knows but certainly not of this year, Lord. The curve is up and down many hours nearly every day— up last night as Thou didst speak through the cool, silent southern stars and the crosses in the sky. Up this sweet morning—O Father, how I love!

SATURDAY 22

II Timothy 4   **Dar es Salaam Club**

SITTING in the church alone for a long while trying to
give Thee out to many people, I *wanted* to become that way
habitually, so that to see a man would be *more* than to pray;
it would be to *give him my soul filled with Thee,* O Christ.
Can I become that way to the English with their insufferable
snobbery? Can I ignore it? Can Love and I draw a circle
to take them in and to understand them and to give my
soul to them full of Christ? That is a good test! "The common" people are easy to love and help. Give me love enough
even for snobs!

This second letter of Paul to Timothy brings tears. Poor,
wonderful Paul! "The time of my departure is come," "All
that are in Asia turned away from me," "Hymenaeus and
Philetus . . . have erred," "Demas forsook me," "Alexander
. . . did me much evil," "Only Luke is with me." He wants
Timothy to "come shortly." O Paul, you tasted the same
desertion Christ experienced! It is necessary to be "made
perfect through suffering." All of us must, sooner or later.

————— • —————

SUNDAY 23

Titus I   **Dar es Salaam Club**

FATHER, am I not learning that the best way to pray
for people is to go and sit near them and pray while there?
Perhaps holding their letters or photos in my hand is as
effective. This experiment which I began May 8 with letters
and photos, recording the hour when I pray, may answer
this question.

Looking at Johnson's African pictures last night, with
the growling lions devouring a zebra and the shrieking
baboons fighting monkeys, then pondering upon "the still
small voice of the spirit," I see that the soul must grow out
of coarse, cruel, dumbness and numbness, like that of a rhi-

noceros, into the sensitive acuteness of the violinist scarce touching his high note. The soul must become like the mystic who hears the whisper of the Spirit.

——— • ———

MONDAY 24

Titus II   Dar es Salaam
                                                      German Pension

GOD, if like the radio, I *am* succeeding in sending out thoughts to other minds, the *real* question is *what my mind tells other minds*. The radio is a great invention, but that music yonder across the street is not worth broadcasting. Every wave of prayer from my mind must say, "Love, sacrifice, Christ, truth, loyalty, faith, beauty of soul, growth toward perfection, surrender, let the spirit of Christ flood your soul, live in the presence of God, help and help and help. . . ." I want the power of broadcasting to grow only when the message is purely and perfectly what Thou dost desire.

Thank Thee for the growing eagerness of the Africans and the ease with which they are learning to read and write. What kindly, lovable souls these Africans are!

——— • ———

TUESDAY 25

Titus 3   Dar es Salaam
                                                      German Pension

FATHER, lonely, surrounded by noise and folly, I *need* *Thee* today. It is an opportunity to try putting more pressure on the will upward toward Thee and outward toward others. Here is a situation to challenge my strength of purpose. A challenge to make the life lived close to Thee joyously attractive to these others! When they speak only German, help me to speak the silent language of Christ. Nothing about self—all about Thee throughout the meal.

As I walked homeward this afternoon through the native section, after teaching in the school, I saw another truth;

63

Thou art ever *eager* to reach out Thine arms and enfold those who are lonesome, the aged whom we all forget, the poor, the obscure little people, when they plead to Thee. The ugly, those with nothing to attract, can nestle in Thine arms.

How often we say this!

Thank Thee for the pain that makes me *experience* it—with Christ. I could not have known it at the Club. How blind, how blind we are!

———— • ————

WEDNESDAY 26

Philemon   Dar es Salaam
                                       German Pension

FATHER, thank Thee for the sleepless hours of last night when I could pray so intensely for so many people. If the collisions of countless electrons produce waves in ether, if our nerves are minute broadcasting tubes, then does the conflict between the will to sleep and a rebellious excitement start waves around the world? Can we sublimate all kinds of mental crises into powerful broadcasts about Thee? Minds touch other minds far away when emotions are working intensely, as in accidents, approaching death and danger, more frequently than at any other time. *Must* feelings be stirred to reach *far?* Perhaps so, we do not yet know; but we *do* know they work that way thousands of times. Thank Thee for every cut, for every hour of loneliness, for every sense of horror, for every struggle of temptation that stirs me deeply, if it also helps me to be Thy radio station to many souls. Anything, Lord, but do not let my soul sleep!

———— • ————

THURSDAY 27

Hebrews 1   Dar es Salaam
                                       German Pension

FATHER, at this large meeting this morning Thou didst prove once more that when I call upon Thee, Thou art always quick to respond. Thank Thee for the privilege of seeing such progress and so much interest, and for leading the way to the best lessons we have ever made. Help, O help me to stay very, very, very close this whole week.

Were those six men just emerging from illiteracy the nearest to Thy heart in all that gathering? God, does Thy heart ache as mine does at thought of the multitudes of little people who have no hope, who are driven to vice as their only source of emotion, for poor stupid girls who see no other way to a life of variety and attention than vice. What a frightful, hideous sin the "righteous" commit in not affording innocent doorways to a more abundant life! And we think we can be "sinless" by staying away from the victims of our neglect!

——— • ———

FRIDAY 28

Hebrews 2   Dar es Salaam
German Pension

FATHER, tired but very happy at the complete success of this African journey, I feel glad tonight at the gratitude and eagerness of the Africans. I am glad to learn afresh that the most rewarding work in the world is to help those whom everybody else forgets. In this town where a line cuts first and second class officials apart, I am glad that I have drifted among "the poorest, lowliest and lost," for almost all of us whites are climbers shouldering or glaring out of our way the very people who need us most. Thank Thee tonight that I never was and never can be a "social success," for, weak thing that I am, I too would doubtless have cut those who need me most—the forgotten, the poverty-stricken, the colored brothers of Thy world and mine, and I would have lost this joy!

65

SATURDAY 29

Hebrews 3   British Residency, Zanzibar

GOD, those three whom I know to be immoral in Dar es Salaam, whom I so wanted to help, and yet whom I left without a word concerning Thee, worry me tonight. Perhaps, if I had reached some more prayerful state, they would have listened. Perhaps my life spoke more than I realized. I think I felt the awakening of their consciences. Is it cruel to make them miserable in those circumstances unless I help them out of their bondage? No, for the end of this life is not happiness found by putting the conscience to sleep. And my prayer can follow them. O love that will not let them go, use my prayer for them.

Thank Thee for these Arabs with whom I am seeking the ideal way of teaching Arabic, and may Thine arms be around us as we work together and get Thy full will accomplished.

——— • ———

SUNDAY 30

Hebrews 4   British Residency, Zanzibar

GOD, the perfection of sainthood lies along one stern hazardous road: complete mastery of one's body; constant effort to improve environment; complete, perfect obedience to the will of God; slave of the Highest, master of the lower. That will mean loving all things lower, not for what they are yet, but for what they may become and for what I may, by love and service, help them to become. Help me to be afraid of no man no matter how strong or antagonistic, but to walk into his mind with my thoughts, carrying the cross of Christ at the heart of my thoughts, and demanding that he surrender to Christ. Tighten up this new habit that I so feebly have tried to cultivate. Starting over now, help me to carry Christ to every soul I meet or think of—Christ, aggressively, tenderly, eagerly, lovingly, irresistably and constantly. *I do not want to forget!* nor make a half success.

MONDAY 31

HOW astonishing is this gospel! The maker of worlds put wee, two-legged creatures on a tiny planet of a second rate sun, put in those wee creatures souls, set these souls free, and then began gently to knock at the doors of their hearts begging them to open and let Him come in and do them greater good! Every second He sustains their lives, sees to the very center—yet cannot enter the inner soul until we open the door. He came and clothed Himself in flesh to woo our affection. He let men torture and crucify His body, He suffered and suffers when men refuse to let Him enlarge and glorify them. This amazing story is just a little beyond our comprehension, and yet we grasp enough of it at times— at those moments when our souls hunger and thirst—enough of it to fling ourselves weeping into Thine open arms, as I do now, O incomprehensible, incredible Love!

June, 1937

TUESDAY 1

Hebrews 6

On Ship at Mombasa
S. S. Takliwa

FATHER, as we press on unto perfection, how can we master situations? How can I learn to hold Thee in mind when, like last night and this morning, I am in a cabin with two other men, or in a dining room talking with people? It should be easier on this ship half full of passengers.

What would *perfection* mean? Perfect *poise,* smooth nerves, perfect control of one's thoughts, perfect mastery of every situation, perfect wide-openness upward to Thee. We need hours of solitude for this discipline. Then, if the *human race* is to achieve this perfection, there must be fewer people, no crowding, wide parks for solitary wandering, spots where men can talk aloud to Thee. This "pressing on toward perfection" is not *perfect* until we press for *world perfection.*

——— • ———

WEDNESDAY 2

Hebrews 7

S. S. Takliwa

AS I turn my back upon Africa, where two months of eager exploring in Dhuluo, Olinyore, Kikuyu, and Swahili brought such fine results, my prayer shall haunt the men and places I have seen. God, *do keep* dear friends in Maseno, Kima, Jeanes School, Alliance, the Italian priests, the directors, the inspector, those Africans with their hearts aching with mine to help their people; and in Zanzibar the Principal, the director, those fine Africans, the Arabs, the Indians, the Jeanes teacher, the Catholic priest, the governor, all of whom have taken some of my heart; in Dar es Salaam, the director and his wife, those fine African leaders, those men

68

and women whom we taught, the teachers of Central School, the great-souled editor of Mamba Leo, the Germans whom I could not reach—and back of them that mighty pitiful, hopeful continent—God, God, God.

"My boy, thank you for sharing Africa with Me in your burdened heart."

—— • ——

THURSDAY 3

Hebrews 9   S. S. Takliwa

AS conversation turned on death yesterday, it set my thoughts upon that adventure. If scientific inquiry *does,* as I believe, support belief in the survival of the soul, if psychic research does bear out the hope that we shall sail forth upon a new, glorious voyage of discovery, then we need to publish all that evidence to help people everywhere. We all need to learn to look forward to that new "awakening from this sleep called life" with keen zest! If I can feel then as I do now, I think I shall step into the next life with positive, impatient eagerness when God has done what He can do with me here. We will not stop working through all eternity. My mother, father, children, Garrett Edwards, Warren Siegfried are still working—especially, I think, my fine dad.

—— • ——

FRIDAY 4

Hebrews 10   S. S. Takliwa

GOD, what was the meaning of that vision last night when I saw a finished gilded or golden inscription—was that a rift in the clouds that told some of Thy story? I cannot remember it now, though I saw enough in a second to fill this page. It was something like this:

"I come to each stage of culture in the form that stage can understand. To the neolithic man I came in neolithic form. . . ." I cannot recall the beautiful words you used to describe all cultures. That tablet must still lie in my memory,

69

and will return when you wish. Did the Koran look like that to Mohammed? Dare I ask such questions? "Yes! That was what the tablet meant. Just that. Be not bound by another man's conception of orthodoxy. I am breaking through to humanity wherever, whenever, however men say 'come,' and I obey no man-made orthodoxy. The one thing of which you can always be sure when you hear a statement about Me is—'God is more than that.'"

—— • ——

SATURDAY 5

Hebrew 11   Seychelles Islands
                                             S. S. Takliwa

THIS eleventh chapter of Hebrews made me catch my breath with the sheer loftiness of its glory. It broke upon me after ten chapters which meant but little. Was it my limitation that brought no responsive fire? Must one experience the great heights in order to understand them? I have lived so much of this chapter! "Being warned of God concerning things not seen as yet. . . ." "When he was called, obeyed . . . and he went out, not knowing whither he went. By faith he became a sojourner in the land of promise." "They were strangers and pilgrims on the earth. . . . now they desire a better country. . . . choosing rather to share ill treatment . . . than to enjoy the pleasures of sin. . . . he endured, as seeing him who is invisible. . . . that apart from us they should not be made perfect." Does the past still need us for its perfecting? Yes! And let me rise above this heat, this strange environment, and live up to that goal! *Now!*

—— • ——

SUNDAY 6

Hebrews 12   S. S. Takliwa

"OUR God is a consuming fire." How honestly do I face that side of Thy nature, God? I have tried to forget all but Thy love and patience because I have fallen so far short of

70

Thy Will. "God dealeth with you as with sons." He chasteneth us "that we may be partakers of his holiness." I have forgotten the "consuming fire" and remembered only Thy "redeeming fire." Ah, My son, read on! "Removing . . . those things that are shaken, . . . that those things which are not shaken may remain." The spirit cannot be destroyed; it can only be purified. What looks like destruction of life from your present point of view is burning out the dross, and preserving the gold. The things that are seen melt away like the waves outside your porthole. The things not seen are eternal. "Let us also, seeing . . . lay aside every weight, and the sin which doth so easily beset us."

—— • ——
MONDAY 7

Hebrews 13   *S. S. Takliwa*

FATHER, when we come heartbroken to Thee, art Thou as I was when this dear little girl came and wept in my arms because she had said "damn." We are all so like that ten-year-old dear. We hear others and imitate them and then cry our eyes out. And didst Thou smile in Thy heart as I kissed her cheek and felt a glad pain with her?

"And to communicate forget not." God, I see that the pathway toward being "perfect in every good work to do his will" must be the entrance of *every* door that helps me *speak* to others. I refused to try to heal that cripple when the Voice said "heal him." I refused to lead the service on my own initiative. I want to stop refusing. I said I was lonesome because a half dozen English people on board are snobs. But this ship is full of Indians and others who need me. God help me to follow the voice into second class and into steerage. Down there they think I am the snob!

71

TUESDAY 8

James 1   *S. S. Takliwa*

AGAIN, the drinking and dancing on the deck has set loose profound depths of intensity which I have sublimated by prayer for friends until my eyes in the mirror blazed black and penetrating. I begin to realize how we need temptation, loneliness, disappointment, pain, failure or some tragedy to draw out these latent powers which otherwise lie dormant. Then, when these conditions are around, we need to know how to harness them for Thee and for our fellow men. Perhaps this year is telling me how to *capitalize* my difficulties. "Count it all joy . . . when ye fall into manifold temptations. . . . that ye may be perfect and entire, lacking in nothing." How far, *how far* I have yet to go! But Thou, O Christ, art standing far up yonder beckoning and smiling. Even Thou wast enkindled with incredible power by the conflict with Thine enemies and by Thy suffering. It is the way to soul-power. "E'en though it be a cross—Nearer, my God, to Thee!"

———— • ————

WEDNESDAY 9

James 2   *S. S. Takliwa*

FATHER, here is my hand. With a sluggish brain I shall let Thee speak through me to this paper if it is Thy will. Where would Jesus wander, what would He do if He were on this ship? Would He remain on first class deck? Surely He would visit the whole ship, giving His benediction as He passed along. They would not need to understand His words, for His love would reach out like a halo and people would feel, as well as see His smile. I gave Thee my hand to write this. Now, Father, here are my feet to walk where Jesus would go, where Jesus will go in me. Here are my lips, here my heart, my love, to be made beautifully Christlike by Thine own Self. And now, if love is pure and unselfish and tender

72

—Christ-filled—we, Thou in me, will make our tour of the other classes.

———— • ————

THURSDAY 10

James 3   *S. S. Takliwa*

WHEN I am in touch with Thee, fruits begin to appear at once as they did yesterday when I had re-surrendered everything. And when I am not consciously and wholly yielded, then appears resentment at English snobbery. All the while the really important factor was my own unlikeness to the warmhearted Christ. Looking back to my college days and since, I now believe all my social failures have been failures to possess enough of the love of Christ, failures to abide every moment in the vine. "Apart from me ye can do nothing." That is no pious platitude—it is a grim key to failure. I have been so hideously selfish and touchy and divided and weak away from Thee that *I do not want to forget* to make every minute a new surrender. Here is my will. Do not let me have it back. I hate that ugly, separated self. Apart from Thee self rots!

———— • ————

FRIDAY 11

James 4   Conscious 80%   *S. S. Takliwa*

THIS week had almost passed when I had such an unusual opportunity to concentrate upon Thee. Yet only one day was over 70%. And Thou knowest how almost fiercely earnest I was yesterday morning! And I know the reason —I have kept it a secret. The two who saw this diary last week helped me greatly. I thought nobody on the ship this week would understand. That was fear and lack of faith. This I have learned at least—I cannot keep my secret. Somebody on this ship must share it today. Perhaps showing this diary to people must from today onward become a part of the

73

experiment. Praying for people is not enough. I cannot keep Thee. I cannot keep surrendered to Thee except when I am giving Thee away. But now, to whom? Father, lead me.

—— • ——
SATURDAY 12
James 5   Arrived 7:00 A.M.
                                          Bombay Harbor [India]

THANK Thee for the response of that sailor to this diary, for the responses of all three to whom I have given it, and for the wonderful way in which the whole day changed. I have learned that I cannot go about praying for people or trying to keep Thee in mind when I am not *doing* all I can to help, to share, to teach, and to lift. Piety cannot be a substitute for works and for witness. Thank Thee that sharing this book has thus far proven a blessing to those who received it and to me who shared it. Now, as I go ashore, help me, O help me, God, to step through every door toward which Thy finger points. Take these four faculties that matter most—my eyes to look for need, my ears, my tongue, my brain. *Spirit Christ* melt into me from head to foot—love!

—— • ——
SUNDAY 13
I Peter I   C.M.S. Building
                                          Proctor Rd., Bombay

THANK Thee, Father, for the wonderful letters that came yesterday. The past still lives and speaks to the present, through letters as well as through memories. We *are* building day by day an invisible temple. All of those past days are bricks in the temple. Those events *do* make us what we are today. I feel like shouting to the whole world this morning: "Watch today very jealously. It will rise again to bless or curse you." Youth does not know this, does not know how true are the words of Jesus. "Nothing is hidden that shall not be revealed." Perhaps the judgment day may consist of exhibiting that temple built by our past to the hosts of heaven to make them praise or shudder! No, that cannot be, for evil must not enter heaven. But the perfect Christ will help us finish our perfect temple.

—— • ——

MONDAY 14

I Peter 2

C.M.S. Building
Bombay

TOMORROW, Father, begins the last fifteen days of this, the most earnest and glorious six months of my life. Yet not one day has been a complete success. Even had I remembered Thee a whole day, there would have been heights beyond of perfect surrender, perfect subjection of ugly, little self, perfect thinking *only* Thy thoughts, perfect loving service of others, perfect disdain of color or caste or education, so that I should go out on the street overflowing with Christ-love, exhaling it as the *dama de noche* fills the air with her fragrance. Those Himalayas of the Spirit-life help me realize what a mean, low person I am—and these all about me. But we can rise! We are rising! God, let us get our teeth into this day and see what we can do with it. No forgetting! No fearing! No refusing! No yielding to heat or tired feelings! Just a day full of "Yes, Lord, yes!"

—— • ——

TUESDAY 15

I Peter 3   Conscious 75%   Girls School
Sholapur

LIFE is to fill these white pages for fifteen more days. There aches in my breast a painful longing to write *wonderful* days in this and in the *higher book of Life. Be present,* be Master each ticking second! Every thought toward Thee or, better still, from Thee every moment.

These six months have taught me how I must *make* an environment that constantly reminds me. This little crucifix,

75

a gift of gratitude, and my thinking of Jesus in an empty chair beside me, are good reminders. Praying for an hour yesterday for all in the car was a great help. My telling my secret to others made yesterday one of the sweetest days of my life. I *must* tell it on every occasion.

Thank Thee for Margaret Sangster's *Little Letters to God.* She knows the secret! Thank Thee that such a soaring soul can get into secular journals. We can never overcome evil by denunciations. We must flood the world with glory drawn out of God's own heart, and make it irresistible!

—— • ——
WEDNESDAY 16
I Peter 4   Home of Rev. F. C. Sackett
Secunderabad, Hyderabad State

Conscious 95%

THIS day, a higher percentage than any before it, is so rich I could write pages! What enabled me to keep Thee in mind all day? First, praying for these thousands whom I passed. Second, telling Mr. Sackett about my experiment at the *very first* opportunity. Third, reading *The Disciple Whom Jesus Loved* by Lofthouse. Fourth, talking aloud *to* and *from* God. Fifth, a resolute "No" to books and scenes that might break the endless contact with God. Sixth, a picture of Christ on this wall. Seventh, Mr. Sackett bringing me two books, *Letters of Samuel Rutherford,* and *Quiet Hours* by Fulsford. How strikingly those for whom I prayed in the bus responded today! Is my spirit perhaps becoming incandescent when Thy full current is on? When they turned and looked, should I have spoken? "The perfect Father and the perfect Son, each of them revealed in the other, while into that relation the human race is intended itself to enter." That, says Lofthouse, is the thing no other religion ever thought of. Into that relationship we are invited. What glowing glory feeds my soul!

76

THURSDAY 17

I Peter 5   Home of Rev. F. C. Sackett
                                         Secunderabad, Also Medak

FATHER God, direct this mind and these fingers. The interest shown by the servants in Sholapur proves these little globes of the world to be fine for opening *the subject*. Thank Thee for the miracles of today—the miracle that brought me far out to this rural station of Medak, among lovely Christians and prepared this marvellous committee to drop all other work and join in preparing the new Telugu lessons; for the amazing progress made in one day, for the growing ease with which it was possible today to witness.

Here, Father, is an earnest prayer for the illiterate men and women who studied today. May this begin the *life of glory in Christ* for them, and for all the depressed multitudes joining the church. May surrender be complete, their souls undying fires of devotion, their minds wide with Thy world vision! (7:00 A.M.)

———— • ————

FRIDAY 18

II Peter I   Medak, Hyderabad State

DEAR God, telling others about my experiments in practicing Thy presence, is the best of all aids to success. Would this new upsurging of power have come at all without the pouring out of all I had last night? "Go ye into all the world, and preach the gospel to every creature," for you increase by sharing and lose when you refuse. What folly this fear has been all these many past lost years! Teach us followers round Thy little world to be afraid of neither man nor devil, but to be afraid of one thing only, refusal to take every chance to *tell it*, tell what matters more to *us* and *them* than all the world besides. Make us quick to see open doors, quick to

77

enter them, and tenderly loving with a gentle, considerate, imaginative, selfless ability to share with others. (7:30 A.M.)

—— • ——

SATURDAY 19

II Peter 2 Medak

THIS miracle of being led here where they all so need help, of seeing this committee formed without previous notice, the finest committee we ever had, of seeing fifteen excellent lessons in Telugu emerge in two days, with duplicate copies of each, takes one's breath.

The sight of that magnificent Medak Cathedral, the finest Christian church in India, out on these plains, symbol of the permanence of Christ in India, built by all the poor people's money and loving labor, is another miracle. God help Indian people to pack the walls and atmosphere of that cathedral with the glory of perfect surrender. Make it Thy Spirit clothed in cement and stone! Here, God, take all of me You can use and use me to help that church to exhale Christ!

—— • ——

SUNDAY 20

II Peter 3   Conscious 85%   En route to Bangalore Mysore

FOR this book of Kerr's, *The Vision of God,* I thank Thee, Father, because it contains some nuggets of pure gold. "Unbroken, personal intercourse with the Divine is the end for which man was created; a foretaste of this experience is possible even in this life." "For final *self-forgetfulness,* the whole attention of the soul must be centered upon the most absorbing, the most inspiring and the most perfect of objects." *Final self-forgetfulness*—is that necessary for perfection? Perhaps. But self-forgetfulness is not attained by severe self-discipline. It will be a fact when Thou hast come to absorb all our thoughts, when every thought is from

Thee or to Thee. So let us begin instantly! *Now*, what is Thy voice saying, as Thou speakest in a million ways? "Witness, My child, tell the *one story* all the world needs to know. Tell everybody everywhere without a moment of hesitation."

———— • ————

MONDAY 21

I John I   Bangalore

GOD, my conscience troubles me; too many situations have defeated me. I am afraid of people. Yesterday I thought I could find no way to begin speaking of Thee to those men on the train. High above me Himalayas of character show me how far down I still am. The very fact that this worries me, while all about are so many thousands who probably have not yet even begun to try, shows how low I am. *This* is not self-forgetfulness. Please, please, God, do Thy thinking here, Thy world thinking, as Thou art lovingly brooding over Thy two billion souls. What, God, would be a good way to open the question of Christ? Is this not a major problem for timid Christians? We cannot stop after praying for people, for if we pray only, we soon cease to do even that. There must be a fine balance of prayer and service and witnessing.

———— • ————

TUESDAY 22

I John 2   Bangalore
                                    Missionary Rest Home

GOD, bless the old people who look back upon their best days with wistful longings. Help them to understand that even ninety-one years is but infancy for the soul, and to look ahead with eager expectancy to the more glorious adventure that lies ahead.

As one hears of the collapse of the Church Union plans in India and the onward sweep of the Oxford Groups, does it mean, God, that perhaps these old shells are too cold, too hollow to matter much, and that a new outpouring of Thy spirit can flow only with a new fulness of surrender? If so, then perhaps such vital movements as the Oxford Groups may put Thy spirit into the present churches, for where Thou art, O Christ, there is the church.

———— • ————

WEDNESDAY 23

I John 3

Bangalore
Missionary Rest Home

MORE miracles! until one expects them daily. That the director should appear one minute after I called, that he should find such an excellent aid at his side to help, that this Methodist Normal should be eager to aid and so swift, that the drawing master should be so competent, that Miss Swift should be able to call the missionaries so quickly, and many other happy facts reveal Thy hand working, Father. And this marvellous chapter, tenderly exclaiming, "Behold what manner of love the Father hath bestowed upon us, that we should be called sons of God. . . . Beloved, *now* are we children of God. . . . we shall be like him. . . . And every one that hath this hope set on him purifieth himself. . . . Hereby know we love because he laid down his life for us: and we ought to lay down our lives. . . . Let us not love in word, neither with the tongue; but in deed and in truth." There is the trouble with our age—we did not practice what we professed; then we doubted, supposing our faith to be false because *we* were false to our faith.

———— • ————

THURSDAY 24

I John 4

Madras
Railroad Station

ENOUGH to write a book this morning! This supremely glorious chapter four of First John: "God is love." "Let us love one another: . . . every one that loveth is begotten of God." "He that abideth in love abideth in God. . . . There is no fear in love: but perfect love casteth out fear . . . he that feareth is not made perfect in love."

For that splendid gathering of missionaries and their sympathetic interest, thank Thee, and for those two ardent Oxford Groupers who took me to dinner and poured out their radiant witness of how utter surrender had changed them and changed the prostitutes whom they are rescuing. They are right; a really transformed world must well up out of a transformed humanity. The Oxford Groupers have gone to the heart of reality as few others have. They seem like old friends.

—— • ——
FRIDAY 25
I John 5   Madras Y.W.C.A.

AS thousands of people watch the Dionne Quintuplets from behind special glass windows, seeing the children but unseen by them, perhaps we, too, are "surrounded by a great cloud of witnesses" who see through a one-way screen what we do and what we think. Are they watching—father, mother, children, Mayor Phillips? How the list suddenly swells! Are they looking through the one-way window as we play our game with minutes? We must play it as though sixty-thousand unseen rooters wanted us to win, would be wounded, as love only can be wounded, when we fail. Perfect *abiding in His arms* and minute by minute obedience to His will is the goal. Thank Thee, Father, for Cecil Rose's *When Man Listens.* These Oxford Groupers have taken in earnest three simple fundamentals—God has a plan, God speaks, man must listen and obey anything God says.

—— • ——
SATURDAY 26
II John   Madras Y.W.C.A.

THIS book, *Testament of Man,* in which Arthur Stanley

tries to illustrate the spiritual experiences of all ages, shows that spiritual threadbareness is the characteristic of this age. The book deliberately omits a wealth of glorious experiences that could fill ten volumes, while this New Testament speaks from every page rich glorious spiritual food for the soul. And this *When Man Listens* glows with Thy Spirit. We need fresh, daring spiritual discoveries, whole continents of them, and we need them terribly. We need a new wideness, a world-wideness. When men will to see God only through the narrow slit science may offer, they see nothing but an "oblong blur."

Thank Thee, Father, for the grave of Annie Besant, and that speaking sunset, and the whispering trees, and that lovely shadow on the water haunted with seekers after Thee.

———— • ————

SUNDAY 27

III John   Train to Trichinopoly
                                        En route to Colombo [Ceylon]

I SEE clearly that we can *accomplish* what we are and not more. Opportunities come and go so swiftly that we must seize them instantly or never. Thank Thee, Father, for the high plane struck in the first moment and sustained in Madras, where so much depended upon that first moment. That high level leaves a pure, sweet taste in the mouth of one's memory. But in retrospect I see how that a nobler I might have entered doors I did not then see. Thank Thee, dear Lord, for all the precious friendships in Christ which spread over India and Africa. Today it seems to me the only *sure* supporters of literacy are those tied to my soul by Thee. And those who know the most about my aspiration seem closest even though they have not revealed themselves to me as I have to them. We must get into one another's souls and find the hidden best. We must learn to make everlasting friendships—in three days, or even one!

MONDAY 28

Jude

GUIDANCE yesterday and today *did* work as the Groupers said it would. Thank Thee, Father, for the way contact
with them has put an edge on my conscience about witnessing. Why did it seem so hard and hopeless to witness to
that circus man and prize fighter last night, until he himself opened the subject of religion? Why did he do that
twice? Make my witness stronger, surer. Perhaps it does not
require much talk if it is accompanied by prayer. Thank Thee
that he showed his great gratitude for the Oxford Group
book. And how Thou hast guided this forenoon: to the
newspaper, the Y.M.C.A., the director, the principal of the
Training School, and other places. Thank Thee for leading
me back to Effa—make me a constant joy and uplift for her.

——— • ———

TUESDAY 29

Revelation I   Conscious 80%   *S. S. Potsdam*

AS I looked into the mirror over this desk, I did not see
a face at all like the dear dreams that have flooded my mind.
There are no ugly wrinkles like that on the forehead of
my soul. One's face keeps dragging behind all the per-
plexities and strains and clashing desires of a lifetime, and
also the long lifetime of that mysterious call that came up
for a million years and passed to me through my parents.
That mirror does not tell the truth about my soul today. And
when I walk this deck, I do not see souls as they *are* or
will *become,* but only distortions dragged up from the past.
Help me, Father, to see their future and help it to become
true! Here is another wistful prayer for India, where I have
seen Thee working so many miracles. It is sweet to share
the eager longings which fill Thy breast for India, and the

breasts of thousands of Christ-filled Christian missionaries. God use me to send them new joy.

———— • ————

WEDNESDAY 30

Revelation 2   *S. S. Potsdam*

THE last morning of the best six months inwardly and outwardly of my life, up to this time, finds me, Father, appreciating the Oxford Groups. We are running on parallel lines. To be a Grouper I should not need to change at all in seeking Thy guidance, or in writing a diary! I shall have to struggle harder for absolute perfection in purity, honesty, unselfishness, and love. Could I find a trusted friend and tell everything in my past—could I? That would be a humiliation. But was it not exactly what St. Augustine's *Confessions* tells all the world? God, I am willing when Thou commandest; but Thou wilt desire me to help him who hears, not harm him. The Group is ahead of me also in witnessing, and I shall need to carry that burden closer to my heart. But do I not have something to contribute from these six months: (1) the game of keeping Thee in mind every second, (2) praying for every person I meet or think of, (3) learning Thy language, and so understanding what Thou art saying every moment. These are some of the lessons and rewards of the past six months of struggle and glory.

A Final Word

So ended the 1937 diary. It was a daily record of an effort to hear God's instructions, minute by minute, and to carry them out in a new, creative field which was far beyond my own abilities. I am sure God did through us what none of us who worked together could have done alone and without Him. The foundations were being laid for a literacy program which has since spread far over the world.

All of us had the sense of being caught up in a purpose we only dimly understood. Everywhere we were under a strange excitement. I am sure there are periods when God needs us for important purposes, and keeps pushing us and calling us and helping us to reach His goal. We did not realize in 1937 what stupendous changes were taking place and were yet to take place in the world. Looking back, one can now see that universal literacy is necessary for the world that is now emerging. God was using us to help prepare illiterate men to read His Word. The Bible is the most important Word that God has ever recorded. Nearly two thirds of the world could not read that Bible in 1937. Today it looks as if education will, indeed, become universal.

How much of that strange, wonderful experience of God's help was due to the fact that *He* needed *us* to help Him? How much of it was due to our own earnest, spiritual quest? I really do not know. I think God gave us that passionate hunger to do His will as well as that wonderful fulfillment. When one has an intensely earnest desire to carry out the will of God, God can then get his messages through and His work accomplished.

Of course, if this is true at all, it is enormously important. It is of all truths the most needed by a floundering, groping world. Everybody wants to improve himself or his position in life, but most individuals are trying to do it alone. They soon discover that they cannot lift themselves by their own boot straps. Yet they do not know how to reach up and grasp the hand of God.

Spiritual discoveries are not like discoveries in the physical world. We may all observe an experiment in physics or chemistry, but we cannot look into the mind of another person and see the secret and infinitely complicated thoughts which come and go. All we can do is to describe to one another what goes on within ourselves. This is why those who are undertaking spiritual pilgrimages ought to keep daily diaries and make them available to one another, especially if they make exciting discoveries.

I am sometimes asked whether I continued the spiritual voyage recorded in *Letters of a Modern Mystic* and in this book, *Learning the Vocabulary of God;* and if so, what were the results. The answer is that I never stopped—and I now suspect that you and I shall never cease taking voyages and making discoveries through all eternity. My explorations down through the years have followed a large variety of directions, almost every direction on the compass. I find that in 1942 I was fascinated with the question, *How to listen?* Here are some memos from that period:

—— • ——

SATURDAY, JULY 4, 1942

Luke 8:21

GOD, there are two ways to listen to Thee. One is passive, like those who enjoy an opera—with emotion but no action. The other way is active—when we are alert to receive our orders from Thee and to obey. Then we offer not only our heart and mind but also our *strength* to Thee. Both ways are right when we use them at the right time. Frequently when we are passively listening, Thou dost send a message about something we must do. Then we must do at once what Thou commandest. I resolve to listen *much more* and to rush around in nervous futility *much less.*

—— • ——

SUNDAY, JULY 5

John 14:15-18

GOD, wisdom and knowledge come to those who listen

86

to You. Those who "wait upon the Lord" are opening their lives to the very fountain source of all wisdom. We who are trying this way of getting knowledge find that our listening hours are rich with inspiring things to write or say or do. Only when we hold our ears close to Your lips do we have this sense of a sudden invasion of a divine idea.

God, you talk to us through our best thoughts. Lovely ideas are your whispers, even though we may never suspect that they come from You. I am sure that every step forward in my life came as an idea while I was looking up with the eyes of my soul, waiting to be "stirred by the invisible."

As the years passed, I have found that *obedience* to God's voice is even more difficult than *hearing* Him speak. I find in my 1950 diaries scores of pages on how to make obedience absolute. I was having more trouble with a rebellious will than with a deaf ear. It became clear to me then that even Jesus Himself *earned* the complete *confidence* of the Father, so that all things could be entrusted to Him, by total, constant, unwavering, glad, instantaneous obedience. Jesus says: My meat is to do the will of Him that sent me." John quotes Jesus as saying: "If any man willeth to do his will he shall know." Jesus knew perfectly because He was perfectly willing to know. One could not know if one were not willing to obey; the moment the willingness was perfect, the answer would be there. That is what I believed in 1950. But I am not so sure today that this is the last word.

Many people down through the centuries have believed that they were absolutely right, but today we are convinced that they were absolutely wrong. The world is full of such people, who are convinced, but wrong. Indeed, I suspect that by this time next century people will say that we are *all* wrong in our dependence upon military force. We try to force our convictions upon men who try to force their convictions upon us. One of the chief causes of disputes and war is that men have such deep convictions that they fight and kill men with equally deep convictions—all of them sure that they are right!

How shall we prevent ourselves from holding *wrong convictions?* One way is to seek the advice of many people of quite diverse opinions. That may help us to face all the facts.

But then everybody may be wrong! Often whole nations are.

If, as we believe, Christ *is* the *way*, the *truth* and the *life*, then one way for us to see with a clear eye is to saturate ourselves day after day in Christ and His teaching, to walk with Him across the pages of the four gospels until we instantly and instinctively look at every question from His viewpoint. Then His word that bears on every question will leap to our lips.

The other way is to *consult* Christ; to talk directly to Him. I heard Roland Brown tell a dream he had had. He saw that his mind was far larger than the confines of his skull. Indeed, it was a vast room. There was a knock at the door of his mind. He opened the door, and there stood Jesus.

"Come in. You are welcome," said Roland.

"I cannot come in," said Jesus, "unless I can sit on the throne of your mind and become your King."

"Come in and take the throne, and be my King forever," said Roland.

Then Jesus came in and sat upon the throne and directed Roland's life and thoughts and will.

Instead of thinking by ourselves, it is a fascinating adventure for you and me to try whether we can acquire the fixed habit of looking to the King on the throne of our minds to supply every thought and to initiate every act.

Talking everything over with the King and accepting His decisions is a wonderfully exhilerating, relaxing happy way to live. He ceases to be like a King and becomes a warm, close, affectionate brother, as He was to His disciples.

Jesus said, "My mother and my brethren are these who hear the word of God, and do it."

CPSIA information can be obtained at www.ICGtesting.com
Printed in the USA
BVOW08s2016291115

428779BV00003B/57/P